The Doctrine of the Church

The Doctrine of the Church

DOW KIRKPATRICK, editor

Prepared Under the Direction
of the World Methodist Council

ABINGDON PRESS • New York • Nashville

THE DOCTRINE OF THE CHURCH

Library of Congress Catalog Card Number: 64-15757

SET UP, PRINTED, AND BOUND BY THE PARTHENON PRESS, AT NASHVILLE, TENNESSEE, UNITED STATES OF AMERICA

Preface

THE YEARS SINCE WORLD WAR II HAVE SEEN AN UNPRECEDENTED INTERnational flow of persons and ideas. This flow has been in two directions—one in the direction of the ecumenical church and the other in the direction of world confessional bodies.

There has been a creative tension between the two sufficient to give both movements vitality and to result in productive cross fertilization. The Methodist Church, in fashion similar to other denominations, has sought to enrich its theological contributions to the world Church through a renewed effort of self-understanding.

Twice—in 1958 and 1962—Methodist theologians from over the world have met each other at Lincoln College, Oxford, of which John Wesley was a fellow, for a period of doctrinal inquiry and encounter. The third such theological institute is planned for the summer of 1965.

The results of these studies contribute to an awareness on the part of the denomination itself, of its self. Then, primarily through the participation of the individuals, the stimulation of theological study within Methodism is hopefully expected to contribute constructively to the ecumenical church's thought and life.

The present volume is a symposium on the doctrine of the church, resulting from the 1962 Oxford Institute on Methodist Theological Studies. This contribution from a Methodist source will add greatly to the discussions on the subject by the entire world Church.

It will be immediately obvious that Methodists have no "party line" to offer, even if one were wanted. Perhaps the most helpful result from such a volume as this would be to create widespread discussion and writing as vigorous as the discussions at Oxford which followed the presentation of each paper. All over the world are Methodists whose lifetime vocation is teaching, writing, and preaching theology. Apart from this Oxford Institute they have had little or no personal contact with one another. It is not their remoteness from one another, however, which has produced the variety of their accents. It is rather the mood of the Methodist mind to be independent. It is, therefore, not to be expected that the simple device of bringing these persons together will result in narrow agreements. Rather there is produced that creative ferment which it is hoped will be stimulated in the total church by these present contributions.

There are certain unities, however, which become quite evident in these studies. The major one is the strong biblical context sought for all these inquiries. The general theme of the 1958 Institute was "Biblical Theology and Methodist Doctrine." So throughout 1958 and 1962 there is a constant examination of the biblical basis of the doctrines which have come down to the modern church through the Reformation and the Wesleyan Revival.

This fact gives hope in two directions. Certainly as long as Methodist contributions to the world Church's studies of theology are biblically based, we will be in the best position to offer unifying theology rather than divisive. Further, the biblical milieu may be a more effective ground of communication with the modern world than we have believed, as Dean Trotter points out in Chapter 11.

The manner in which modern Methodist theologians hold John Wesley is instructive. Wesley studies, especially in the United States, have been so accelerated during the past fifteen years as to amount to a revival of a dead interest. Wesley is studied extensively, genuinely appreciated, but held loosely. The extremes of scathing sarcasm on the one side and canonization on the other are avoided. The more he is studied the more he is seen to be not the accidental historical factor which produced another denominational separation, but one of the true mentors of the whole Christian community along with names well known in the early Reformation Church. Here again Methodist scholars discover an ecumenical ground in his writings which can be as meaningful for any Christian thinker as for a Methodist Christian.

The development of this theme in this volume is believed to be a fresh approach to the subject. The discussion of the opening question by Albert C. Outler goes immediately to the crux of the whole question of Methodist self-understanding and ecumenical relation. C. H. Dodd, C. K. Barrett and E. Gordon Rupp set the biblical and historical perspective of the question.

The direction of the study is then shifted to deal with baptism, confirmation, ordination, the Lord's Supper, and other early Methodist means of grace. The result of this section of the study is that the two Protestant sacraments are studied not as Methodist sacraments, but as Methodist views of Christian sacraments. The questions of confirmation and ordination offer an opportunity for parallel studies of the laity and the ministry.

The volume closes by pointing the theology of the Church off in the two directions it must go to be relevant in our time—church unity and appeal to modern man.

There are obviously many open questions not dealt with here—relations with the Roman Catholic Church, the role of the Church in social redemption, and the Christian Church in a world of non-Christian religions, secular history, and science. Again may the hope be expressed that the appearance of this symposium will generate through the world of Christian thought considerable discussion and reaction.

Extraordinary assistance has been given in getting these chapters into print by Dean William R. Cannon of the Candler School of

Theology, Emory University, Atlanta, Georgia, a member of both the 1958 and the 1962 institutes, and by Dr. Philip Watson, of Garrett Theological Seminary, Evanston, Illinois, a member of both Institutes and author of one of the chapters of this volume. The Rev. A. Raymond George, Wesley College, Headingly, Leeds, not only was a member of both Institutes and a contributor to this volume, but also served with me as joint secretary of the institute committee. To these persons we are indebted, but they carry no responsibility for any shortcomings of the symposium.

Expressions of appreciation to all the authors must include the statement that they have willingly made their contributions to the institute and to this volume freely. An especial word of gratitude is extended to Dr. C. H. Dodd, the only non-Methodist and to Dr. Harold Roberts, Principal of Richmond College, and immediate past president of the World Methodist Council, who served the institute as its warden.

—Dow Kirkpatrick

Contents

1

Do Methodists Have a Doctrine of the Church?

ALBERT C. OUTLER

In the way it is posed here this question is a trap for the unwary. The answer "yes" says too much; "no" says too little. "In a manner of speaking," which is more nearly accurate than the other two, seems, nevertheless, equivocal. Like many another formally indeterminable question, however, this one is important and it becomes more poignant at every new turn of current church history. Far from being an academic affair amongst ourselves, the shape and thrust of Methodists' notions about the church and about themselves as churchmen have deep and wide repercussions, not only in the management of our own internal affairs but in our relationships with the rest of the Christian community in our time.

Thus, I was willing to undertake what I recognized as an ambiguous assignment—not because I have an unambiguous answer to offer or the "true doctrine" of the church to propose. The discussion of this question is useful only because it unfailingly bestirs a cluster of cognate questions, the consideration of which might serve to illuminate what I take to be our real problem: Methodism's place and mission in the current situation of Christianity-in-crisis. The following comments, therefore, are intended to provoke reaction—less to themselves than to the problems they point to. I am far less interested in winning your agreement than I am in the possibility that you may be provoked, even if in a contrary fashion, to join with me in the basic reconsideration of Methodist ecclesiology which our present circumstances clearly require of us.

Nor have I tried to guard each sentence from the embarrassment of specific qualification and possible amendment. Overcautious lectures make for dull discussions. It might be well, however, to make the otherwise impertinent comment that what is here presented is actually less impromptu and impressionistic than its rhetoric may suggest to certain proper academics!

In the beginning the people called Methodists had no distinctive doctrine of the church—for the very simple reason that they did not need one (and it is a clear rule in church history that Christians do not *think*—i.e., construct doctrines—unless they *have* to). The early Methodists were not a church and they had no intention of becoming one. They understood themselves to be one among a number of religious societies and revival movements in the eighteenth century dedicated to the salvation of souls and the cultivation of the Christian life in its utter seriousness. The specific terms of membership in these societies had no *ecclesiological* reference ("to be saved from their sins and to flee from the wrath to come"), and this by design. The overwhelming majority in the United Societies were already nominal members of the Church of England or had at least been baptized therein. John Wesley was a stanch churchman—prepared to be irregular and inconsistent but also to defend his irregularities and inconsistencies on what he took to be *Anglican* principles. Charles Wesley was an actual bigot on the point of conformity. Such ecclesiological notions as the rank-and-file Methodist may have had were strange mixtures of attachment to and alienation from the national church.

This meant that if they had no fully formed or peculiar *doctrine* of the church, they did have a peculiar *problem* in and with the church to which they were related—that is, the Church of England. In its simplest terms, it was the problem of how to be an evangelical order (or society) within a "catholic" (or quasi-catholic) church, which steadfastly refused to sponsor or even to sanction their order and their enterprise. In the last meeting of this institute, Professor Shipley summed up the early Wesleyan conception of a *ministerium extraordinarium* within the *ministerium ordinarium* of the Church of England. It was *this* notion of being divinely commissioned "extraordinary messengers" which provided the frame for the characteristic organization and program of the original societies. Wesley could "look upon all the world as his parish" because, as he explained in a letter to James Hervey, "thus far I mean, that in whatever part of it [the world] I am I judge it meet, right, and my bounden duty to declare, unto all that are willing to hear, the glad tidings of salvation. This is the work which I know God has called me to. . . ." In similar vein he could say to his lay assistants: "You have but one business: that of saving souls." It was this limited but central objective that justified the Methodist ecclesiological irregularities—field preaching, lay preaching, Wesley's extra-parochial, supra-diocesan pattern of supervision and control, extemporary prayers in worship, et cetera. Moreover, it justified the Methodists' continuing existence as a religious society within the Church of England, despite the latter's massive disapproval of them. It was on this principle that Wesley deliberately designed the pattern of Methodist preaching services so that they would be liturgically insufficient, leaving the Methodist people still dependent on the priests of the national Church for the sacraments and the full round of Christian corporate life. Wesley never tired of insisting: "We are *not* Dissenters; we are *not* Sectarians; we will not separate!"

But what were they—these people who were in but not of the eighteenth-century Anglican establishment? They puzzled and offended many an Anglican leader—both the good ones, like Butler and "John Smith" and Edmund Gibson—as well as the bigots, like

Lavington and Warburton and Church, who raised the cry of "enthusiasm" and let it go at that. Moreover, the Methodists were a sore puzzle to the Dissenters, who could not understand why such vigorous advocates of holiness would not "come out from among [the corrupt national church] and be separate." It was, therefore, inevitable that as time went on an increasing number of Methodists—though always in a minority—began to regard their situation in the Church of England as anomalous and intolerable. But Wesley knew what the Methodist societies were intended to be and he set himself to make and keep them so; an evangelical order defined by their unique *mission:* "to spread scriptural holiness over these lands."

Once he was involved in it, the revival dominated the rest of Wesley's life—his preaching, theologizing, writing, publishing, his private and social affairs. He was convinced that the Methodist societies were the chief human agencies of the revival—and that this was their importance and justification. They were also his hope of reforming the Church of England—not by overthrowing the establishment or even capturing it—but by their actual performance of the church's essential mission, where this was going generally by default. Whatever else Methodism ever was or has since become, its first and most decisive identification was as an enterprise of Christian mission, witness, and nurture.

John Wesley's own doctrine of the church, like the rest of his theology, was an interesting amalgam. Its solid, consistent core was hewn from bedrock deposits in the Anglican tradition, laid down by the tradition of anti-Roman English "catholics"—such as John Jewel and Richard Hooker. For example, the decisive motifs of Jewel's ecclesiology, as seen principally in his controversy with Thomas Harding, may be summarized under five heads: (1) The church's subordination to Scripture; (2) The church's unity in Christ and the essentials of doctrine; (3) The notion that paradigmata for ecclesiology should be drawn from the patristic age; (4) The apostolic doctrine; (5) The idea of a *functional* episcopacy (as belonging to the church's well being rather than its essence). Each of these motifs re-echoes in Wesley whenever and wherever he refers to the *form* of the church and to its *continuity in historical existence*. The grounds on which Hooker justified and approved continental ordinations are precisely those on which Wesley proved to his own satisfaction that an *exclusively* episcopal polity was not original or classical Anglicanism.

Wesley's view of the church as *a community of liturgy and devotion* was framed from such diverse sources as the Catholic Nonjurors (Hickes, Kettlewell, Ken, Nelson) and the Puritan masters of devotion (Scougal and Baxter). His ideas about the form and administration of the church came, not from the Puritans nor the Dissenters, but from the so-called *latitudinarians* (Stillingfleet, Lord King, Tillotson, *et al.*). Wesley's vision of an evangelical society serving the church almost against its will was a creative synthesis of Anthony Horneck's vision of a church reformed by "religious societies," from the Lutheran and Moravian pietists, from the fourth-century seekers after the perfection of the Christian life, and from the Society of Jesus—about which he had curiously mixed feelings. His sacramental theology was borrowed outright from his father's *Pious Communicant*—from which he took his *Treatise on Baptism*—and from Daniel Brevint's *Christian Sacrament and Sacrifice*. The influence of the continental Reformers in this particular area is never more than indirect—and that from the Protestant moderates (Bucer, Peter Martyr, Melanchthon) mediated largely through Cranmer (*Homilies*), Jewel, *et al.* This goes with his generally dim view of Luther, his *implicit* rejection of Calvin's concept of the New Testament model of the church, and his *explicit* rejection of the sectarian ecclesiologies of the Protestant left wing.

The three primary texts for what we might call Wesley's *resultant* ecclesiology are Sermon LXXIV, "Of the Church"; LXXV, "On Schism"; and the *Minutes* of 1745. Important auxiliary texts are his sermon "On Numbers 23:23" and the one on "The Ministerial Office." To readers of this volume a detailed exposition of these texts would be impertinent, but there are certain accent points which I would like to recall in the framing of the basic hypothesis of this chapter.

The catholic or universal church is *coetus credentium*—the entire company of men and women whom God hath called out of the world to give them the power of living faith. The Church of England is that part of this whole company who are inhabitants of England. In this connection Wesley affirms the *positive* meaning of Article XIX but then goes on to reject its negative implication—for, strictly construed, the article excludes members of the Church of Rome from the church catholic, and this Wesley was unwilling to do.

In the sermon "On Schism" Wesley distinguishes between *diversity* amongst Christian groups, and *disunity*. The New Testament sense of "schism," he maintains, is neither more nor less than an alienation of Christians from each other in heart and love—even "though they still continued members of the same external society." Such a "division of heart" may, however, lead to or occasion "schism" in its common usage: "*causeless separation from a body of living Christians*. . . ." "It is only when our love grows cold that we can think of separating from our brethren. . . The pretences for separation may be innumerable, but want of love is always the real cause; otherwise, they would still hold the unity of the Spirit in the bond of peace."

To those who urged that communion with the Church of England was in itself corrupting—and so concluded, "You ought to separate from the Church of England"—Wesley replied:

> I will make the case my own. I am now, and have been from my youth, a member and a Minister of the Church of England; and I have no desire nor design to separate from it, till my soul separates from my body. Yet if I was not permitted to remain therein without omitting what God requires me to do, it would then become meet and right, and my bounden duty, to separate from it without delay. To be more particular: I know God has committed to me a dispensation of the gospel; yea, and my own salvation depends upon preaching it. . . . If then I could not remain in

the Church without omitting this, without desisting from preaching the gospel, I should be under a necessity of separating from it, or losing my own soul. . . . But, setting aside this case, suppose the Church or society to which I am now united does not require me to do anything which the Scripture forbids, or to omit anything which the Scripture enjoins, it is then my indispensable duty to continue therein. (Sermon LXXV, "On Schism.")

In the *Minutes* of 1745, and in connection with the question of his own status as chief pastor and bishop of the Methodist Societies, Wesley thus summed up his concept of church *polity:*

The plain origin of church-government seems to be this. Christ sends forth a preacher of the gospel. Some who hear him repent and believe the gospel. They then desire him to watch over them, to build them up in the faith, and to guide their souls in the paths of righteousness. Here then is an independent congregation, subject to no pastor but their own, neither liable to be controlled in things spiritual by any other man or body of men whatsoever [so far, bare-bones, bed-rock Congregationalism].

But soon after some from other parts, who are occasionally present while he speaks in the name of Him that sent him, beseech him to come over and help them also. Knowing it to be the will of God he consents (complies), yet not till he has conferred with the wisest and holiest of his [original] congregation, and with their advice appointed one who has gifts and grace to watch over the flock till his return [in his absence].

If it please God to raise another flock in the new place, before he leaves them he does the same thing, appointing one whom God has fitted for the work to watch over these souls also. In like manner, in every place where it pleases God to gather a little flock by his word, he appoints one in his absence to take the oversight of the rest, and to assist them of the ability which God giveth. These are Deacons, or servants of the church, and look upon their first pastor as their common father. And all these congregations regard him in the same light, and esteem him still as the shepherd of their souls.

These congregations are not strictly independent. They depend on one pastor, though not on each other.

As these congregations increase, and as the Deacons grow in years and grace, they need other subordinate Deacons or helpers; in respect of whom they may be called Presbyters, or Elders, as their [common] father in the Lord may be called the Bishop or Overseer of them all. (John Bennett's copy of the Minutes of the Conference of 1744, 1745, 1747, 1748. Publication of the Wesley Historical Society, No. 1. London, 1896. Published for the W. H. S. by Charles H. Kelly.)

This is, of course, a quite fanciful account of the actual history of the first and second centuries of the Christian Church. It is, however, an almost exact account of the rise of Methodist Societies from 1739 to 1745—and of Wesley's understanding of his own role therein.

The story of the long struggle over separation is gnarled and knotted. I do not myself know all of the requisite data for its intelligible rehearsal. As far as I know, these data do not exist in any accessible form. Nobody has ever put together Wesley's testimony with the corresponding testimony of both his opponents and partisans. There are, however, visible salients in the story—the conference of 1755, where John barely averted a determined push toward separation; Edward Perronet's mischievous doggerel in *The Mitre;* Charles Wesley's horror of separation and his subsequent withdrawal from the revival (on *this* score more than any other); the increasing clamor of the lay preachers to be treated as equals to the ordained clergy. These serve partially to account for the fact that "separation" was a perennial issue, renewed at *every* annual conference of which we have a record from 1755 to 1790.

Shortly after the conference of 1755, Wesley wrote to a fellow evangelical clergyman, Samuel Walker (September, 1755), in defense of his evangelical order within the Church of England, "irregularities" and all. His main point with Walker is that these so-called irregularities are, each one, functions of the evangelical mission of Christian witness and discipline—and are not necessarily symptoms of dissent. What he would very much like to negotiate, he says, is "a method . . . which, conducted with prudence and patience, will reduce the constitution of Methodism to due order, and render the Methodists under God more *instrumental to the ends of practical religion.*" (Italics mine.)

In all these comments—and everywhere else that I know of—

we find the essential *notae ecclesiae* characterized in a distinctive way. This is what I would call the *classical Methodist* [Wesleyan] *ecclesiology:*

1. The *unity* of the church is based upon the Christian *koinonia* in the Holy Spirit.

2. The *holiness* of the church is grounded in the discipline of grace which guides and matures the Christian life from its threshold in justifying faith to its plerophory in sanctification.

3. The *catholicity* of the church is defined by the universal outreach of redemption, the essential community of all true believers.

4. The *apostolicity* of the church is gauged by the succession of apostolic doctrine in those who have been faithful to the apostolic witness.

Significantly, and at every point, Wesley defined the church as *act,* as mission, as the enterprise of saving and maturing souls in the Christian life. This vision of the church as mission was to be realized and implemented within the Anglican perspective of the church as form and institution. Moreover, Wesley took some pleasure in appealing from Anglicans drunk to Anglicans sober—from Butler to Jewel, from Lavington to Cranmer, from Warburton to Hooker—and from everybody to the *Articles,* the *Homilies,* and the Book of Common Prayer!

The Methodists did become a church, however—after all and on their own—by a complicated process which it is partisan to defend and fruitless to deplore. For what it is worth, I might remark in passing that I feel acutely embarrassed as a Methodist who is also a historian, because of the lack of an adequately critical, adequately comprehensive rehearsal of British or American Christianity in the half century from 1790 to 1840—and of Methodism's role in that history. Such a thing would be a very useful contribution to modern church history and to ecumenical understanding. It might supply yet more evidence for the thesis of C. H. Dodd's now famous letter about the "*non-theological* factors" that have complicated and frustrated the quest for Christian unity.

What we can say, however, is that Methodism's transition from society to church came in the bright morning of the branch theory of the church, when the analogy of competing business companies made good sense to Christians as a parable for the rivalries of their several sovereign and autonomous "denominations." Moreover, the evolution of Methodism as a denomination proceeded under circumstances which have engendered lasting bitterness between Methodists and Anglicans—exacerbated by the atrabilious tempers of the Tractarian controversy. The effect of this was to push the Methodists into the arms of dissent with something like enthusiasm, so that they came quickly to be almost indistinguishable from the other free churches in most observable respects.

The historical patterns of this transition from society to denomination are tangled and vary widely from country to country and from time to time. It first began in the U.S.A., then in Great Britain and elsewhere. One of the most interesting instances was in Canada, where the evolution of Methodism took yet another course from that in the States or in Britain. This needs to be understood if the later development of the United Church of Canada is to be understood. In every instance, however, the transitional process involved a series of borrowings and symbiotic adaptations. Typically, when Methodists have felt a lack in matters ecclesiological they have looked about for whatever seemed handy and truly useful—and then proceeded to adapt it to their own uses and purposes (often quite different from the original). Examples of this sort of thing in American Methodism are (1) "episcopal polity," (2) the scheme of representation and delegation in the conference system, (3) the written Constitution of 1808, and (4) the patterns of frontier expansion and settlement. In England (or so it seems to an American who is scarcely expected to understand such things—really!) Methodists came to be increasingly so far estranged from the Church of England (for reasons that have varied from pique to righteous indignation) that they found themselves readier to adapt to the patterns of dissent and sectarianism. This tendency in Methodism after Wesley to borrow from left and right gave rise to a theory of the church as a *coincidentia oppositorum.* As William B. Pope put it,

To [the church] there are certain attributes assigned. . . . These qualities are Unity, Sanctity, Invisibility, Catholicity, Apostolicity, Indefectibility, Glory. But we also find by the side of these . . . qualities in some measure their counterparts or opposites: such as Diversity, Imperfection, Visibility, Localisation, Confessionalism, Mutability, and Militant Weakness. Hence we gather that the true church of Christ is a body in which these opposite attributes unite. (*A Compendium of Christian Theology,* III, 266-67.)

One way and another then, Methodism in the nineteenth century evolved from an evangelical order in a catholic (or quasi-catholic) church into a low-church Protestant denomination or congeries of denominations, but always with subtle differentiations from its congeners—those groups which were more nearly linear descendants of the continental Reformation. As firmly committed as other Protestants to *sola Scriptura,* the Methodists were also "Arminian" and anti-antinomian, and thus never *quite* like the "reformed" traditions in their interpretation of *sola fide.* The theological consequences of this were very considerable—as Dale Dunlap has shown in his Yale dissertation.

In America the Methodists were low church to begin with, differing violently with the Baptists—and later the Campbellites—on such matters as "believer's baptism," immersion, and "the connexional system," but becoming very similar to them in many other respects; e.g., in social typology and ethos. In the present century—for such are the vagaries of ecclesiological ecology—the well buckets have reversed themselves, and now American Methodists have been drifting toward congregational autonomy at a great rate, while the Baptists and the Christians are on their way to becoming almost as "connexional" as the Methodists used to be. Moreover, there are both Baptist and Christian congregations which now "dedicate" infants—and a great many Methodists who "baptize" them with what looks and sounds as if it were the same basic theory of what is going on, or *not* going on! At the same time, however, both

British and American Methodists still preserve selected, mutilated remains of the Book of Common Prayer for various ritual and ceremonial purposes. In the current revival of interest in liturgical reform a good deal of it is patently imitative. My point is that if we are to understand the anomalies of Methodist ecclesiology—or anything else doctrinal in Methodism—we must take this deep-seated symbiotic tendency into account.

Nevertheless, in this history of being a church without having been intended to be one, there are landmarks which remind us that Methodists, when they really face up to the task of self-understanding, usually recover their racial memory of the evangelical order which once upon a time was raised up on an emergency basis to extend and deepen the reach of the gospel witness in uncommissioned service to the church's essential mission. To do the work of the church in default of the church's being the church in its ideal fullness—if we take Richard Watson and William B. Pope as exemplary, as on this point I think we can—we quickly discover that, for each of them, ecclesiology is an auxiliary concern claiming very little of their genius or originality, which is devoted in large measure to what might nowadays be called "the theology of evangelism."

For Watson the first business of theology is to exhibit the derivation of doctrine from revelation—and so to connect the preaching of the gospel with its source. The bulk of the *Institutes* (Part I) is devoted to the authority of the Holy Scriptures and to "Doctrines of the Holy Scriptures" (Part II)—with "Redemption" (II, xix-xxix) the vital core of the entire system. In "The Institutions of Christianity" (Part IV) he expounds a view of the church as a spiritual fellowship of believers which should never be "established" but must have powers of government and discipline—all of them *functional.* Baptism is interpreted—as in Samuel Wesley—in covenantal terms, to be administered to infants, and normally by sprinkling. As for the Lord's Supper, he concludes that Article XXVIII, in its 1662 version—and without certain particular expressions in the liturgy—"must be taken to be the opinion of the Church of England upon this point, and it substantially agrees with the New Testament" (II, p. 667).

For Pope the heart and center of Christian truth is soteriology, and this as grounded in the atonement and expressed in the Christian life of faith and holiness. Pope's doctrine of the church is frankly eclectic and mediating—taking the Anglican *Articles* in their pre-Laudian interpretation, but interpreting their consequences in a staunchly "non-conformist" temper. His liveliest comments come when he describes the church as the organ of the Holy Spirit and the matrix for the maturation of faith. Here he homes in on the Methodist class meeting (in one of his rather rare positive references in *The Peculiarities of Methodist Doctrine* [1873], pp. 18-19):

Throughout the world, but especially in Great Britain, the Methodist people hold fast the tradition of a Christian communion which confesses the name of Jesus not only before men generally, as in the Eucharist, but in the assemblies of the brethren themselves. Not that we have a monopoly of this kind of fellowship. Meetings for mutual confession, and edification and counsel have always been aimed at in the purest ages and purest forms of the Church; but *we are the only community that has incorporated them in the very fibre of our constitution.* Growing out of our society character, this institution we have aimed to interweave with the organization of the Church also: not yet with perfect success but with results that encourage *the hope of perfect success.* As it is rooted in our ecclesiastical economy, so it is rooted in the affections of our people. No form in which the social element of Christianity has found expression has enlisted more universal enthusiasm in its favour than the old class meeting. Other forms of confederation have been gloried in, lived for, and sometimes died for, in the history of Christendom. But I question if any institution, grafted on Scriptural precepts, has ever commanded such widespread and pervading homage of all orders of the devout, or approved itself by such practical and irresistible evidences of good, as the Methodist class-meeting. . . . Incautious and unskilful hands have been meddling with it of late; but in vain. It may admit of much improvement in detail and in administration, but its foundations are secure and inviolable.

Would to God he had been right on this last point!

In the twentieth century Methodism, in America at least, has undergone a radical metamorphosis which naturally affects any ecclesiological reflection that goes on within our ranks or about us by others. It is an oversimplification in the direction of the truth to say that this was chiefly the effect of German-Enlightenment theology assimilated into a tradition which had lost its vital traditionary linkage with classical Methodism. One way of describing the outcome of this development would be to say that we have passed beyond the gravitational field of our historical origin and are now in what might be called a condition of weightlessness as far as our peculiar history is concerned—a detraditioned state of mind and polity. In America at least, Methodism is an "established church" (in the sociological sense) in which the maintenance and expansion of the establishment has become an undeclinable prime duty for almost everyone associated with it.

Ecclesiologically speaking, however, we are a church after the order of Melchizedek. Estranged from our Anglican heritage—for reasons that range from cogent to paranoid—having no blood ties with any other mode of catholic Christianity (as the Lutherans and Calvinists have even in their *anti*-Romanism), and having become too "worldly" and middle-class a movement ever to make genuine common cause with the "radical Protestants" and the Pentecostalists, we are churchmen whose institutional forms are uniquely our own but whose theological apparatus has been assembled from many quarters—whose "place" in the ecumenical movement is painfully equivocal.

For all this derivative and symbiotic behavior there remains a deep, almost instinctive awareness among us that our foremost and final justification for being the church that we are is still precisely the same as the justification for our having first been an evangelical order within *ecclesia Anglicana*—namely, Christianity in dead earnest, distinguished chiefly in our evangelical concern for the Christian mission, witness, nurture—"holiness of heart and life." I cannot myself point to any contemporary ecclesiological formulation or formula that I would now acknowledge as *the* "Methodist doctrine of the Church." But I honestly think I can recognize a constant and comparatively consistent concern amongst Methodists that strikes me as characteristic and "peculiar." The Church is "a company of faithful men" (i.e., *men with a mission*) "in which the Word rightly preached [evangelism] and the sacraments duly administered" [worship], together with everything else that is relevant and requisite to getting the rightly preached Word truly heard and the duly administered sacraments rightly received (Christian *discipline,* or nurture). Our *notae ecclesia* are, therefore, evangelism, worship, discipline. It interests me to notice that whenever the motif of *the mission of the evangelical order* is mentioned in an assembly of Methodists, it strikes a responsive chord, even if in contexts that are sometimes faintly bizarre. In the crucial and profound debates over the issues currently paramount in the Faith and Order Commission of the World Council of Churches, for example, one sometimes gets the impression that the Methodists are not really listening—at least, not with their "third ear." But when someone speaks incisively about the church in essential action, even the most overinstitutionalized Methodist in "the connexion" snaps to attention—and feels at least a fleeting impulse to report for duty.

The drift of these comments is that Methodism has never lost the *essence* of a *functional* doctrine of the church but that, by the same token, it has never developed—on its own and for itself—the full panoply of bell, book, and candle that goes with being a "proper" church properly self-understood. This makes us *une église manqué,* theoretically and actually. But this raises the question of our relations to other denominations, which is to say our ecclesiastical "foreign relations"—those which we maintain within the pan-denominational pattern of the World Methodist Council or those we share in the interdenominational patterns of the World Council of Churches (and, *mutatis mutandis,* national and regional councils of churches).

It is by now a commonplace that the ecumenical movement is

one of the great facts of current Christian history. It is also common knowledge that Methodists have had interesting difficulties in finding and taking their place in the full round of the operations of the World Council of Churches. In the process some fairly stupid stereotypes have emerged which go on generating or perpetuating what the psychiatrists call a parataxic relationship between Methodists and non-Methodists. I, for one, am rather weary of them, but they continue to haunt us at conference after conference.

I have suggested that there is not now, and there has not been for at least two generations, even a modicum of a *consensus fidelium Methodistica* in ecclesiology. In respect of the ministry, more Methodists would agree on the main issues relating to the minister's *role* than on the theological basis of the ministerial *office*. As for questions about apostolicity, catholicity, episcopal polity, the meaning of ordination, and the power of the keys in discipline and excommunication, et cetera—there is no recognizable consensus anywhere and no conceivable prospect of one.

Thus, in America at least, Methodists still practice infant baptism by effusion—but the vast majority would balk at both the premises and consequences of Wesley's *Treatise on Baptism* if they were confronted by it. As for the Eucharist, there is a wide area of confusion in respect of the nature of sacramental grace and on God's presence and action at the Table of the Lord.

As Methodism goes on being—and having to be—a church it will be increasingly harassed and embarrassed by the consequences entailed in the tension between *ecclesia per se*—institutional maintenance and management—and *ecclesia in actu*—proclamation, nurture, and service. If this continues for the next half century as it has for the last, we shall be in a sorry shape for sure. If we go on borrowing and patching and playing with pious gimmicks, we shall not only become ridiculous in the eyes of yet older *poseurs* in our divided Christian family, but our proud claim to a valid heritage may very well become suspect.

One of our difficulties, I suggest, is that Methodism's unique ecclesiological pattern was really designed to function best *within* an encompassing environment of *catholicity* (by which I mean what the word meant originally: the effectual and universal Christian *community*). We don't do as well by our lonesome as some other denominations appear to do—and for a good reason. Preoccupation with self-maintenance distracts us from what is actually our peculiar *raison d'etre*. This is why a self-conscious and denomination-centered Methodist is such a crashing bore to all but his own particular kith, kin, and kind.

Methodism arose as a divinely instituted project—*ad interim!* There can be no doubt that the Wesleys, and most of the early Methodists, understood their enterprise as the effort to meet an emergency situation with needful, extraordinary measures. As with the eschatological views of the New Testament Christians, the "emergency" has lengthened and the "emergency crew" has acquired the character of an establishment. But we lose perspective whenever we forget that we are still more deeply rooted than we realize in the motifs and spirit of the eighteenth-century origins. We need a catholic church within which to function as a proper evangelical order of witness and worship, discipline and nurture. Yet, it is plain to most of us that none of the existing unilateral options are suitable alternatives to our existing situation. The way to catholicism—i.e., Christian unity—is *forward*—toward the *renewal* of catholicity rather than in *return* to something that has lost its true status as truly catholic. Meanwhile, since we *are* a church, it is more than a practical convenience that requires of us that we try to act responsibly in the exercise of our churchly character. This means, among many other things, the reconsideration of our own traditions and their role in that *traditionary process* by which Christianity lives and maintains its authentic continuity with the Christian past and its openness to the ecumenical future. It also means a major reconsideration of the obligations we have as a church in respect of *catechetical instruction,* in more adequate provision for group discipline and therapy, in the ministries of the general priesthood and of the meaning of our own representative priesthood. Almost above all else, it means the acceptance of the liturgical and sacramental obligations of being a church for so long as God requires it of us, pending a really valid alternative of authentic Christian unity.

Every denomination in a divided and broken Christendom is an *ecclesiola in via,* but Methodists have a peculiar heritage that might make the transitive character of our ecclesiastical existence not only tolerable but positively proleptic. On our pilgrimage toward the actualization of the unity in Christ that God has given us and still wills for us to have, we can take both courage and zest from the fact that what we really have to contribute to any emergent Christian community is not our apparatus but our mission. Meanwhile, however, we must ourselves beware lest, in this business of having to be a church while "waiting" for the Church that is to be, we should deceive ourselves by falling further into the fatuity that this business of "being a church" is really our *chief* business!

2

The Biblical Doctrine of the People of God

C. H. DODD

The writings comprised in the Canon of Scripture, extremely various as they are, differing in standpoint and outlook, and spread over a period of several centuries, are bound in unity by their consistent reference to the history of a community, self-identical through many changes. Hebrew clans, Israelite kingdoms, Jewish dispersion, catholic church—all these are successive embodiments of the one People of God. This interest in the experience of an actual concrete community, rather than in abstract philosophical doctrines, is a part of the character of Christianity as a historical revelation. Its theology is essentially an interpretation of what happened in history, with corollaries drawn from it.

The community came into existence at a definite point of history through an act of God. So its members always believed. Traditionally, a body of serfs of the Egyptian crown won their freedom and migrated by way of Sinai to Palestine, and these, with perhaps other kindred clans, formed a religious bond through which in the end they became a nation. These events were understood by those who experienced them in terms of divine election, call, and covenant. There is no reason to suppose that these ideas were imposed upon the memories of the events at a later period. No doubt they meet us in the Bible in developed and enriched forms which we owe largely to the prophets, but the experience of being chosen by God, called by him, in covenant with him, was intrinsic to the events themselves, without which they would not have been what they were. It seems to be a firm element in the tradition and, so far as we can judge, a historical fact, that Yahweh *became* the God of Israel. He was not, like Chemosh of Moab, the virtual personification of the spirit of the tribe, nor, like the *baalim* of Canaan, a virtual personification of the natural powers resident in the land. That he was often conceived as an ordinary tribal god or as one of the *baalim* is clear enough, but always under protest from those who stood for the permanent and dominant tradition. Yahweh *need* never have been the God of Israel at all; Israel was not necessary to him; he was not inseparably bound up with its fortunes. This was a matter of great significance for the riper development of the religion of Israel, since it kept open the possibility that Yahweh might have purposes and designs transcending the national interests, whereas Chemosh (for example) could in the nature of things have no interests beyond those of his people Moab. If, then, Yahweh was not *ab initio* the God of Israel why did he become such? The only answer was that it was by his free and unconditioned choice. There was no more to be said than that Yahweh willed it so. "Yahweh thy God hath chosen thee to be a people for his own possession above all peoples that are upon the face of the earth. Yahweh did not set his love upon you, nor choose you, because ye were more in number than any other people"—nor, we may fairly add, because they were more intelligent or more virtuous or because they had (as it has been put) a "natural genius for religion" —"but because Yahweh loveth you." The idea of a chosen people can, of course, be perverted, and has been perverted, in the service of horrible doctrines of racial and national domination. In itself, however, it is integral to the idea of a historical revelation, since anything that happens in history happens *now* and not then, *here* and not there, to *this* person or group and not to that. This is what has been described as "the scandal of particularity." If in any given case we ask why this and not that, I do not see what account can be given of it except that the Ruler of the universe willed it so. He chose *this* time, *this* land, *this* people for the revelation of himself, and what it means is that no one must ever suppose that he belongs to the people of God through any achievement or merit of his own. Membership of God's people is *sola gratia,* and was never on any other terms.

We have, however, to add that the divine election enters history through a "call" delivered to the chosen people—normally delivered through a chosen individual who can speak with authority in God's name (such as Moses or another prophet), and it is in the response to that call that election becomes effective. This lies behind the idea of the "covenant" which God made with Israel. Our use of the term needs to be guarded, for the English word might be understood to mean an agreement arrived at by bargaining between equal partners. This is in Greek συνθήκη, but the Hebrew *berith,* when it is used of God's "covenant" with Israel, is rendered διαθήκη, a term which carries in it the idea of "ordinance," or "disposition." This emphasizes the divine initiative and supremacy in the whole transaction. Of his own free will God entered into a binding obligation toward Israel and called upon them to accept the reciprocal obligation on his terms, not theirs. "I will take you to me for a people, and I will be to you a god." The response of men to the call of God is taken up into the total act of divine election, and thus a permanent relation is established.

The People of God, then, is a chosen people, an "elect" people. Elected—to what? Not to privilege, prosperity, or dominance. This stubbornly held misconception the prophets had most assiduously to combat. Israel is elected to *responsibility* before God. They have been chosen for the high but perilous destiny of "hearing the word of the Lord," and by covenant they are under obligation to obey his law. Disobedience is disastrous just *because* they are a chosen people. "You only have I known of all the families of the earth; *therefore* will I visit upon you all your iniquities." Thus the word of God becomes a word of judgment upon his chosen people. But it is also a word of mercy, for God himself is bound by his own covenant with the people he has chosen. "He will not fail thee, neither destroy thee, nor forget the covenant of thy fathers which he sware unto them." The word of the Lord as a word both of judgment and of mercy is a theme that runs all through the Old Testament. The tension between its two aspects is perhaps never fully resolved there. The prophets having in their minds the pattern of the true people of God, entirely obedient to his law, and having at the same time the spectacle of a disobedient people before their eyes, sometimes felt compelled to draw the logical conclusion: Israel must perish. Yet Israel cannot perish because God is their God. Ezekiel made a picture of it: Israel was dead. Its bones lay scattered over the valley, and "behold they were very dry." But the dry bones came to life at the blast of the wind which was the breath of God. Thus the theme of death and resurrection entered organically into the idea of the People of God.

So far it might seem that the end to which the whole process was directed—election, call, and covenant—was conceived wholly in terms of the destiny of Israel itself. Disciplined, chastened, punished, even destroyed, by the fearful calamities which were the judgments of the Almighty upon their sins, Israel would yet be restored, purged, made into a righteous nation, and finally glorified; in glorifying his chosen people God would be glorified, and thus his purpose would be fulfilled. There is indeed much in the Old Testament which would seem to justify such a view—and even more, perhaps, in noncanonical Jewish writings. But this is not all there is. As we have seen, the fact that Yahweh became the God of Israel by his own free choice left open the possibility, at least, that he had purposes of his own reaching out far beyond the destinies of Israel. This is never altogether forgotten, even when it is concealed by the distasteful chauvinism of some parts of the Old Testament. The prophets were well aware that Yahweh's first concern is for righteousness, and Israel's calling was, in the last resort, instrumental to this end. They became increasingly aware that righteousness is not a national but an ecumenical interest. Israel, in fact, was chosen to be the instrument of a purpose which transcends Israel. There are hints of such a conception of Israel's calling in many passages of the Old Testament. It comes to clearest expression in the Second Isaiah, where Israel, as the Servant of Yahweh appointed to suffering for his sake, is to be "a light to the nations." With this the idea of election receives its necessary completion, and the "scandal of particularity" is removed.

This cursory survey of the teaching of the Old Testament—inevitably, even absurdly, defective, but I hope not misleading—enables us to envisage what we may call the "marks" of the People of God. We now observe that in the New Testament these "marks" are consistently attributed to the Church—a people elect and called; within God's covenant; the recipient of his Word, now made flesh; bound to obey him; the object of his judgment and mercy—it is unnecessary to catalogue in detail the whole body of attributes transferred directly from the Old Testament to this emergent community which calls itself, in fact, "the Israel of God," *sans phrase.* It asserts without qualification its continuity with the historic Israel of the past and claims all that past as its own heritage. Yet it asserts with equal conviction and fervor its discontinuity with all that has gone before. Its members live in a "new creation": τὰ ἀρχαῖα παρῆλθεν, ἰδοὺ γέγονεν καινά (which, by the way, does not mean—as the K.J.V. has it—"all things [*scil.,* the same old things] are become new," but "new things have come into being"). "The old order has gone, and a new order has already begun" as the N.E.B. reads. The covenant by which it is bound is a καινὴ διαθήκη. The law which it must obey is "a new commandment." And if we have regard to the historical situation it does indeed appear that there was an emphatic, indeed a tragic, breach of continuity at the crucial point. Then is the claim to the heritage of ancient Israel no more than a kind of legal fiction? If not, where are we to find the link of continuity?

In discussing this question, Paul drew attention to the prophetic doctrine of the "remnant"; i.e., the doctrine that when the nation as a whole was disloyal to Yahweh and in breach of covenant with him a minority which remained faithful was vested with the privileges and responsibilities of the covenant, becoming in fact the true Israel within an apostate nation—an *ecclesiola in ecclesia*—and that in and through this faithful remnant, however small, the purposes of God for Israel are carried forward to fulfillment. Such a doctrine might well provide for the emergence of a new Israel which, being affiliated to the old through a tiny remnant of the faithful, has a legitimate right to the inheritance. Did the Church, in fact, arise in this way?

We have to observe that in practice the "remnant" idea worked out in a process of exclusion. It began with the harsh intolerance of Ezra and Nehemiah, who formed the repatriated exiles into a compact little group devoted afresh to the God of Israel, excluding from the reconstituted community all who did not measure up to their own interpretation of the Law. By successive purges they sought to preserve their own purity and so to be worthy of divine favor. Again the exclusive principle manifested itself in the intense devotion and the jealous separatism of Chasidim and Pharisees, with their contemptuous rejection of the *am ha-arez*. Recently we have become aware of a hitherto little known example of an *ecclesiola in ecclesia*—the monastic community of Qumran, fanatically devoted to the idea of a purified Israel, sure of themselves as the men of the covenant and fiercely exclusive of all others. Attempts to affiliate the early Church to Qumran—or to any similar group—are idle. The note of all such movements was exclusiveness, membership of the People of God being restricted to an ever-diminishing minority who could claim to be "righteous." The logic of the "remnant" idea is crystallized into merciless dogma in the apocalypse of Ezra: "Those who perish are more than those who shall be saved . . . almost all are marching to perdition and their teeming multitudes are bound for extermination" (*plures sunt qui pereunt quam qui salvabuntur . . . pene omnes in perditionem ambulant et in exterminium fit multitudo eorum*" (IV Ezra, ix. 15, x. 10). But the Founder of the Church expressly addressed his call to the excluded: "I came not to call the righteous but sinners." In his lifetime he was known as the "friend of publicans and sinners," and in his death he was identified with criminals, dying, as Paul put it, under the curse of the law. The foundation members of the new "Israel of God" were not conspicuously "righteous" persons. They did not look in the least like a "faithful remnant"; they were men who had broken faith with their Master and deserted him at the crisis of his fate. They owed their new standing solely to his forgiveness, and well they knew it. They were members of the People of God *sola gratia*. As we have seen, the original election of Israel is conceived as an act of God's sovereign and unconditioned grace and can only be so conceived, but this principle is now exhibited in the most vivid and concrete manner possible in the election of the Church. The very circumstances of its emergence as a community stamp the Church with a character it can never lose; it is a community of forgiven sinners.

We have not yet found the link of continuity between the old Israel and the new. Let us return to the idea of the "remnant." If the working out of that idea in practice may be schematized as a process of progressive exclusion, producing an ever-shrinking minority of the faithful in whom alone the true marks of the People of God are to be found, then there is a sense in which the logical culmination of the whole process comes when a single individual embodies the true Israel in his own person and stands alone. This is the picture which the New Testament presents. To Christ are attributed the titles which designate Israel as the People of God. "Israel is my son, my firstborn" we read in Exodus. Christ is the Son of God, "the firstborn among many brethren." Israel is the Servant of the Lord, called to suffer for his sake, and through his suffering to save many. Christ is the "righteous Servant," who "came not to be served but to serve and to give his life a ransom for many." The "people of the saints of the Most High" appear in prophetic vision as "one like a son of man," and in the Gospels the mysterious title "Son of Man" is the chosen designation of Christ, an individual designation now yet never shedding its corporate implications. The title "Messiah" itself is in the Old Testament sometimes given to Israel as a people, as well as to its ideal priest and king, and in its New Testament acceptation "Messiah" means one who is in himself the inclusive representative of the People of God as well as their Lord. They are "in Christ," as all mankind are "in Adam." Thus Christ sums up in himself the whole history of Israel's past and takes upon himself the burden of its sinfulness as well as its promise of life from the dead. In life he identified himself with the lost sheep of the house of Israel, and in his death with sinful humanity. As Paul put it, "Christ was innocent of sin and yet for our sake God made him one with the sinfulness of men, so that in him we might be made one with the goodness of God himself" (τὸν μὴ γνόντα ἁμαρτίαν ὑπὲρ ἡμῶν ἁμαρτίαν ἐποίησεν, ἵνα ἡμεῖς γενώμεθα δικαιοσύνη θεοῦ ἐν αὐτῷ). Thus the cross of Christ is interpreted as the voluntary acceptance, representatively, of God's judgment upon the unfaithfulness of his people. "In him" Israel met the death which the prophets had declared to be the issue of its rejection of God. In dying thus Christ affirmed that which gives meaning to the whole idea of a people elect and called to be the Servant of the Lord; he alone offers total obedience: "Lo, I am come, in the volume of the book it is written of me, to do thy will, O God."

As the death of Christ is representative and inclusive, so is his resurrection. When the writers of the New Testament applied to the resurrection of Christ scriptural passages which originally referred to the emergence of Israel from what seemed final disaster, they were not merely indulging in arbitrary or fanciful *pesher*. They saw the destiny of Israel as divined by the prophets made concrete and actual in history on Good Friday and Easter Day. The line of continuity from the old Israel to the new runs through death and resurrection. Paul found language for it when he spoke of the

Church as dying with Christ and rising with him into newness of life, which new life is life "in Christ."

The People of God is thus reconstituted solely by relation to Christ. This is perpetually attested and sealed in the two sacraments of the gospel. Baptism recapitulates in each individual member that process of dying and rising again in Christ, through which the new Israel came into being. The Eucharist, the sacrament of the new covenant, is the communion of his body, in which his people are made partakers of his real and historic humanity—his "flesh and blood," as John put it, taking up the familiar Hebrew expression for human nature in its concrete actuality, *basar w'dam.* In both sacraments the Church is brought back to its historical beginnings. Showing forth the Lord's death in remembrance of him, its members in every age stand at the center from which the People of God is re-created, *sola gratia.*

Two corollaries may be drawn: First, the Church is necessarily *one.* The fact of its unity is largely concealed by the manifold divisions which the course of its history, as well as the sinfulness of its members, has imposed upon it. We now speak of "churches" and hope for their "reunion." We are prone to think in terms of adding the several churches together until they coalesce into a single whole. The unity of the Church is not a unity of aggregation, however; it is a personal unity: ὑμεῖς εἷς ἐστὲ ἐν Χριστῷ Ἰησοῦ—εἷς, not ἕν—"one *person* in Christ." Christ, said Paul, "is like a single body, with its many limbs and organs, which, many as they are, together make up one body." Divided we are, but in the moment when in the sacrament of communion we turn back to the place where the new life of God's people began, the essential unity is ever and again renewed and reaffirmed. At that moment we *are* one, not merely in sentiment, not merely in aspiration, but sacramentally, for we have been made partakers of the body of Christ, and Christ is one. We leave the table of the Lord and are at once involved in things that divide us—even before we are out of church—but we know that in spite of them we are one. It is from this center that the empirical unity of the Church must in the end be restored—how, we do not yet know.

Secondly, since the Church is constituted solely by the relation of its members to Christ—their relation simply as men, to him who is the Man, the Adam of a new humanity—the possibility is given of a genuine universality such as was contemplated but could not be realized while the People of God was one nation among others. In terms of the old Israel the limits of God's people might be defined, either exclusively, by a progressively narrowing definition of the qualifications of the faithful "remnant," or comprehensively, by the addition of increasing numbers of proselytes to the Jewish community. There are signs that both of these principles—the exclusive and the comprehensive—were in the minds of members of the early Church, but neither proved workable. Paul swept both aside with his maxim: "In making all mankind prisoners to disobedience, God's purpose was to show mercy to all mankind." It is possible to fix the center about which the new People of God is constituted, but not to draw its circumference. No attempt to define the limits of the Church, either exclusively or comprehensively, proves workable—as we have so often discovered in our discussions about reunion—and in fact no such definition can hold good which stops short of the totality of the human race. The unity of the Church is the unity of mankind. God has purposed, we read, "to sum up all things in Christ." This is the transcendent purpose to which the Church is dedicated. In serving that purpose, and not in seeking any lesser ends of its own, it finds the ultimate meaning of its calling and election as the People of God.

3

The Ministry in the New Testament

C. K. BARRETT

One who approaches this subject after such scholars as—to name only a few—T. W. Manson,[1] Eduard Schweitzer,[2] and Hans von Campenhausen,[3] cannot hope to find much to glean in a field that has already been efficiently and comprehensively reaped. I hope, however, in the following pages to collect some of the most important data and to indicate some of the principles by which they are related to one another.

It has often been pointed out that it is a mistake to consider the ministry in isolation. It ought to be viewed in connection with and, indeed, as an aspect of the Church. This is true. It is, however, possible and desirable to go further than this. Neither ministry nor

[1] *The Church's Ministry* (London: Hodder & Stoughton, Ltd., 1948); *Ministry and Priesthood: Christ's and Ours* (London: Epworth Press, 1958).

[2] *Church Order in the New Testament* (English translation; Studies in Biblical Theology No. 32; London, 1961).

[3] *Kirchliches Amt und geistliche Vollmacht in den ersten drei Jahrhunderten* (Beiträge zur historischen Theologie 14; Tübingen, 1953).

Church is an entity capable of standing by itself; each emerges against the background of the New Testament εὐαγγέλιον the testimony borne to the creative divine act which catches up the past of Israelite history and initiates the new creation, a testimony in which the powers of the age to come are already at work.

The language I have used to describe the New Testament gospel is eschatological, and its appropriateness would be recognized by all students of the New Testament today. The earliest New Testament theology is an eschatology, and it is within the setting of New Testament eschatology that the New Testament Church and the New Testament ministry must be studied. This is true, for example, with reference to such notable ministers as the apostles themselves, as I have tried to show in two earlier articles.[4] As early as Paul's letter to the Galatians it is possible to trace the primitive eschatological understanding of those "who were reputed to be pillars" (Gal. 2:9; cf. 2:2, 6*a*, 6*c*), and the way in which this primitive appraisal of apostleship was giving place to a view which regarded them rather as administrative authorities than as eschatological figures.

[Paul] is prepared to grant, indeed he cannot deny, the unique eschatological status of James, Cephas, and John as "pillars"; they are the indispensable connecting links between the historical Jesus and the community of the New Age. As such they must be consulted, and fellowship with them must be maintained, at almost any cost. Upon them rested the primary responsibility of bearing witness to the resurrection. This responsibility and privilege could never be taken from them; but there was grave danger lest this, their peculiar dignity, should be not enhanced but obscured by their growing authority within the Church, or at least within the Jewish wing of the Church. To this their position as "pillars" gave them no right; it rested upon a misunderstanding of their eschatological office, which should have pointed away from their own human dignity to the crucifixion and resurrection on the one hand, and on the other to the future coming of Christ and the fulfilment of his purposes for men in the kingdom of God.[5]

[4] "Paul and the 'Pillar' Apostles," in *Studia Paulina in honorem J. de Zwaan* (Haarlem, 1953), pp. 1-19; "The Apostles in and after the New Testament," in *Svensk Exegetisk Årsbok* xxi (1956), pp. 30-49.

[5] *Studia Paulina,* pp. 18-19.

So far we see apostleship as a primarily and originally eschatological function capable of misunderstanding and perversion. It is possible to examine this process—de-eschatologization, if the word is tolerable—on a wider field, both by extending one's attention to the apostles in general and by going beyond the limits of the New Testament. I have suggested that there are two lines along which this de-eschatologizing takes place, a Gnostic line and a Judaistic line. The former when it reaches a full-blown, Valentinian stage can be described as follows: The apostles were men who accompanied the Savior on earth.

> But after his death he appointed them to a new status. He did away with the material part of their life, and kindled to a flame the divine spark which resided within them, as within all true gnostics. In this capacity they became the zodiacal powers, lords over destiny, and were thus able to confer on men, or at least on the elect, a regeneration that meant deification. They were, after Christ, the revealing deities who opened and led the way to the supra-lunary sphere, and to spiritual—that is, non-material—union with God."[6]

The Judaistic line of development, on one of its bifurcations, leads to a surprising conclusion: The apostles disappear, being replaced by blood relatives of Jesus, who appear in the role of priest-kings. In a different branch of the Judaistic line the apostles become, after Jesus, the starting point of a chain of tradition.

These observations about the developing conceptions of apostleship will provide us with a starting point. The primitive conception was rooted in the primitive Christian eschatology, and the understanding of apostolic ministry was modified, and sometimes perverted, as the primitive eschatology was modified and perverted. What is true in regard to the apostles and their ministry is true also in regard to the New Testament ministry in its various forms, and if this chapter has any connecting thread to give it unity and coherence it is this: The correspondence between the varying eschatological conceptions of the various New Testament books and

[6] *S. E. A.* xxi, p. 37.

the development of the ministry. If time permitted (and the theme is one to which I hope to return) it might be possible on these lines to distinguish between legitimate and illegitimate lines of development.

The thesis that the development of the ministry is dependent on the flux of Christian eschatology is not a new one, and I may introduce it with a reference to Martin Werner,[7] who has applied Albert Schweitzer's *konsequente Eschatologie* to the elucidation of the history of Christian doctrine as a whole. Werner has a chapter on "The change in the conception of the Church" due to the effect of de-eschatologizing. Both Jesus and Paul expressed themselves in terms of the idea of the community of the saints which was to appear, with the ultimate manifestation of the heavenly Messiah, as the predestined number of those who had part in the glory of his kingdom. "According to Paul, the Messianic Community, which emerged as a historical entity consequent on the Death and Resurrection of Jesus, was constituted simply of those of the *last* generation, who were elected to participate in the Messianic Kingdom, and this was the generation of the Apostolic period." [8] Naturally this conception of the Church was upset by the delay of the *parousia.* What had been supposed to be the last generation was not the last generation after all. The messianic community developed in historical continuity as an empirical Church.[9] This fundamental change brought many others in its train; for example, in the understanding of the Pauline phrase the Body of Christ, in the sacraments, and in belief about the holiness of the Church. Changed sacramental beliefs and a developing system of ecclesiastical discipline carried with them implications for the ministry. A suitable hierarchy was required both for the dispensing of sacramental grace and for the mediating of forgiveness to penitents. The outstanding example of de-eschatologizing may be found in Callistus' use of Matt. 16:18-19, which was "originally

[7] *The Formation of Christian Dogma* (London: A. & C. Black, Ltd., 1957).
[8] *Op. cit.,* p. 271.
[9] *Op. cit.,* p. 272.

spoken of the eschatological kingdom of God and of the Messianic Community, which would be revealed at the end of time," in defense of "the episcopal claim to jurisdictional authority in the Church." [10]

I shall not go further with Werner, though I am convinced that his view of the history of doctrine deserves more serious attention than is sometimes given it. I have two comments to make, which will lead us to the next stage of our study.

1. The first is a theological point. I have no difficulty in believing that many in the first generation of Christians were surprised to find themselves succeeded by a second. It seems to be true that they believed that the *parousia* of Christ and the visible establishment in glory and power of the kingdom of God would happen when they did not in fact happen; namely, in their own lifetime. I do not find it so easy to believe that God was equally surprised—that, like the tower builder in the parable, he proved unable to complete the work he had begun. It is compatible with trinitarian theology to maintain that Jesus himself in his earthly life looked for a speedy consummation of the eschatological process, but that God's plans were cast in a larger mold and on a longer perspective than could suggest themselves to a first-century Palestinian Jew. The theological ferment produced by the delay of the *parousia* was, we may suppose, part of the theological revolution as God himself had all along intended it. The whole process, after all, was marked by reversals of human expectation. The cross itself, the failure of Jesus' public ministry, was one such reversal. The delay of the *parousia,* the failure of eschatology, was another. We cannot say that all the consequences of the delayed *parousia* were directly and absolutely the will of God any more than we can say that all the features of the crucifixion were directly and absolutely the will of God, but we should not treat everything before the delay became apparent as Jesus' and Paul's mistake, and everything that came after it as a merely human attempt to make the best of a bad job, and botch up God's failure. The whole

[10] *Op. cit.,* p. 280.

process, including the delay and the adjustments required by the delay, constitutes the New Testament event.

2. The second point is related to the first, but takes shape as a simple historical observation. Werner dealt with second- and third-century writers on Church and ministry and noted the effect on them of changing eschatology. But the problem caused by the delay of the *parousia* was felt already within the New Testament period, and its effect can be seen in such writers as Matthew, Luke, and John. This is a proposition that seems scarcely open to doubt; must we go further and agree that these—and other—New Testament writers, like Clement of Rome, Ignatius, and later ecclesiastical writers, are witnesses to "primitive catholicism" (*Frühkatholizismus*)?[11] Much here depends upon the definition of terms. That the way in which these New Testament writers look upon the ministry is connected with their changed eschatological perspective is true, but this does not in itself serve to identify Luke with Clement, or John with Ignatius, in regard to the ministry, to eschatology, or to anything else. There is a view of the ministry that is a legitimate development from the first Christian generation, and there is also an illegitimate view. We shall see something of the distinction between the two at the close of this chapter. For the present we may embark upon a historical sketch of the evidence.

There can be little doubt where we ought to begin if we are to gain a historical account of the development of the ministry (and all I have said hitherto has been intended to suggest that such a historical account is theologically as well as historically significant). The only material we can treat with confidence as early is that which we owe to Paul's pen. The gospels are the literary deposit of a later age; they contain traditional material, and some of this, no doubt, is early and sound, but the whole has been seen through the eyes of the post-Pauline generation. The same is true of Acts; however much early material the book may contain, all has been seen in the light of later developments. We are driven back upon

[11] For a brief account of this question, see my *Luke the Historian in Recent Study* (London, 1961), pp. 25, 70-76.

Paul. We must not assume that he gives us a complete picture of the whole of the primitive Church; nearly all the data he gives us are given incidentally. But the Pauline material has the advantage of being contemporary with the circumstances it describes—or, more often, alludes to—and of being firsthand.

Modern discussion of Paul's apostleship may be said on the whole to assume the truth of Anton Fridrichsen's dictum:

> When Paul in Romans introduces himself as κλητὸς ἀπόστολος he characterizes himself as an eschatologic person. He is a man who has been appointed to a proper place and a peculiar task in the series of events to be accomplished in the final days of this world; those events whose central person is the Messiah, the Christ Jesus, crucified, risen, and returning to judgment and salvation.[12]

To this statement, however, should be added that every Christian is an eschatologic person; if any one (τις) is in Christ, there is a new creation (II Cor. 5:17). This is not to say that every Christian is an apostle; apostles have a place of their own in the eschatological process of salvation; but each man has his own place, and no place is a place of privilege free of obligation, service, or ministry. The ark of salvation carries no passengers.

There is thus a universal ministry of all Christians, of which the mark is the universal possession of the Spirit. If any one (τις) does not have the Spirit of Christ, he does not belong to him (Rom. 8:9). The Spirit is both the qualification and the equipment for service in the building up of the community. His own manifestation of the Spirit is given to each man with a view to the common good (ἑκάστῳ δίδοται . . . πρὸς τὸ συμφέρον, I Cor. 12:7). Such qualifying and enabling bestowals of the Spirit are called χαρίσματα; and when in Rom. 12:6 Paul writes ἔχοντες δὲ χαρίσματα it is clear that he is addressing the whole Church, not a spiritual élite or aristocracy. To this observation, however, it must be added that the χαρίσματα are described as διάφορα; every Christian has a gift, but all Christians do not have the same gift. There are distributions of χαρίσματα, Paul says (I Cor. 12:4), though there is but one Spirit, and these

[12] *The Apostle and His Message* (Uppsala, 1947), p. 3.

issue in distributions of ministries (διακονίαι), though there is but one Lord who is served through them all. It is this distinction among gifts and services that makes it possible to speak of "ministry" in the familiar, technical sense.

Rom. 12 and I Cor. 12 are well known as the places where Paul goes into greatest detail in describing gifts and services. It is interesting to note that in each passage his terminology shifts, though in opposite directions. In Rom. 12 he begins with gifts and moves on to persons exercising gifts: προφητεία, διακονία; then ὁ διδάσκων, ὁ παρακαλῶν, ὁ μεταδιδούς, ὁ προϊστάμενος, ὁ ἐλεῶν. In I Cor. 12 he begins with persons, and moves on to gifts: ἀπόστολοι, προφῆται, διδάσκαλοι; then δυνάμεις, χαρίσματα ἰαμάτων, ἀντιλήμψεις, κυβερνήσεις, γένη γλωσσῶν. The form as well as the content of the two lists indicates the very close connection between gift and function.

A different kind of analysis will show that the ministries or services Paul has in mind fall into three groups: (1) Those operated through speech—prophecy, teaching, exhortation, glossolalia; (2) Services of love to the needy—service (διακονία), the healing of disease and working of miracles, sharing out money and other ways of showing mercy (probably the obscure word ἀντιλήμψεις is to be reckoned here); (3) The activity of taking the lead, presiding, (with ὁ προϊστάμενος in Romans we should put κυβερνήσεις in I Corinthians). These three groups of services correspond to fundamental features of the pattern of Christian existence: (1) The gospel, which must be rightly preached, taught, and understood; (2) Action in love, ἀγάπη, the indispensable mark of Christian life; (3) Discipline, through which Christian obedience is contained and becomes concrete. The sacraments have no place in this list, probably because Paul did not think it the special duty of any particular class of persons to administer them. He himself did not regularly baptize his converts (I Cor. 1:13-17), and there is no hint in I Cor. 11 that the Lord's Supper required a president—rather the contrary (especially 11:33, and see below).

The activities listed in Rom. 12 and I Cor. 12 can be paralleled in various places in the Pauline letters, but for our purpose it will be more interesting to follow up the hint at the end of the last paragraph, and consider one or two things that are noticeably absent from the Pauline letters.

The most striking, suggestive, and perhaps surprising observation is that Paul never uses the word πρεσβύτερος "presbyter" (elder). This is the more striking view of the fact that the word was a familiar one in Jewish society in which Paul had been brought up. How far it was current in Palestinian and Hellenistic synagogues cannot be discussed here; its frequent use for Jewish leaders in the gospels is significant. Von Campenhausen has argued that it is not only the word that is missing. "With the institution of elders we enter into a sphere of ecclesiastical thought of a fundamentally different kind, which cannot readily be introduced into or derived from the Pauline picture of the community." [13] A similar view has been expressed by H. Greeven.[14] The point is that the Jewish presbyterate is an essentially backward-looking office which preserves and transmits tradition and applies it to the life of the community. The Christian churches, however, did not live in the past, but in the present and for the future, a present controlled by the work of the Spirit and a future controlled by the hoped-for coming of Christ. Such communities did not value most highly their links with the past, and the special contribution that their oldest members, with the longest memories, could make. It is true that they were interested in the historic figure of Jesus of Nazareth, but for them he was scarcely a figure of the past. His life, death, and resurrection were parts of the present in which they lived. As the Lord, he was their contemporary.

To take this view is not to imply either that the Christian presbyterate, when it did appear, was, like the Jewish, primarily a link with the past, or that the Pauline communities were completely devoid of leadership. A few passages come under consideration here, including the references to the προϊστάμενος in Rom. 12:8

[13] *Op. cit.,* pp. 82-83.

[14] "Propheten, Lehrer, Vorsteher bei Paulus," in *Zeitschrift für die neutestamentliche Wissenschaft* 44 (1952-53), pp. 1-43, especially pp. 40-41.

and to κυβερνήσεις in I Cor. 12:28. With these we may consider the following:

I Cor. 16:15-18: . . . οἴδατε τὴν οἰκίαν Στεφανᾶ, ὅτι ἐστὶν ἀπαρχὴ τῆς Ἀχαίας καὶ εἰς διακονίαν τοῖς ἁγίοις ἔταξαν ἑαυτούς· ἵνα καὶ ὑμεῖς ὑποτάσσησθε τοῖς τοιούτοις καὶ παντὶ τῷ συνεργοῦντι καὶ κοπιῶντι . . . ἐπιγινώσκετε οὖν τοὺς τοιούτους·
I Thess. 5:12-13: Ἐρωτῶμεν δὲ ὑμᾶς, ἀδελφοθ, εἰδέναι τοὺς κοπιῶντας ἐν ὑμῖν καὶ προϊσταμένους ὑμῶν ἐν κυρίῳ καὶ νουθετοῦντας ὑμᾶς, και ἡγεῖσθαι αὐτοὺς ὑπερεκπερισσῶς ἐν ἀγάπῃ διὰ τὸ ἔργον αὐτῶν·

There are close linguistic parallels between these passages. The common use of the important Pauline technical term κοπιᾶν will be observed. The unusual εἰδέναι in the latter corresponds to the imperative ἐπιγινώσκετε in the former (not to the indicative οἴδατε). The ὑποτάσσησθε in I Cor. 16:16 is explained by the ἡγεῖσθαι ἐν ἀγάπῃ in I Thess. 5:13, and the προϊσταμένους of I Thess. 5:12 by εἰς διακονίαν ἔταξαν ἑαυτούς in I Cor. 16:15.

The context in each epistle is also important. The exhortation of I Thess. 5:1-11 ends with the words: παρακαλεῖτε ἀλλήλους καὶ οἰκοδομεῖτε εἷς τὸν ἕνα, καθὼς καὶ ποιεῖτε; and vs. 14, addressing the same "brothers" as are addressed in vs. 12, continues: νουθετεῖτε τοὺς ἀτάκτους, παραμυθεῖσθε τοὺς ὀλιγοψύχους, ἀντέχεσθε τῶν ἀσθενῶν, μακροθυμεῖτε πρὸς πάντας. What this means is that all Christians engage in mutual exhortation and admonition and in loving service to the community, but some Christians do this better and more abundantly than others. This is the meaning of διὰ τὸ ἔργον αὐτῶν; not "Hold them in love because of their office" (though this is how the words are often taken), but "Hold them in love on account of what they have actually done and are doing."

It has often, and correctly, been remarked that in First Corinthians there is no trace of organized leadership. To secure order at the Lord's Supper Paul bade his readers to "wait for one another" (11:33)—not to wait for the presiding minister. When he dealt with the tumultuous prophesyings and ecstatic speech that went on in the Corinthian assemblies he made no appeal to a leader or chairman to see that things are done decently and in order (14:40); it was the business of the church as a whole to see to it that not more than two or three speak with tongues and to test what the prophets said (14:27, 29). Apparently there was no one to whom he could appeal to look after the funds in his absence; each member of the church had to keep what he has saved παρ' ἑαυτῷ (16:2).

Von Campenhausen wrote: "The most striking feature in the Pauline conception of the community is the complete absence of any juridical order, the exclusion on principle of any kind of formal authority within the local community." [15] This is an important observation and one that carries conviction; it is, however, important to add that this conclusion rests not on the absence of ministries (unless this word is taken, as I do not take it, to mean hierarchical ministry), but on the character of the ministries that are in fact visible in the Pauline communities.

We have seen that the word πρεσβύτερος is absent from the Pauline letters, and we need not linger long over the ἐπίσκοποι and διάκονοι of Phil. 1:1. Older interpreters commonly took the former word in the sense of the presbyter-bishops of the Pastorals, and there is much to commend this view in the fact that when, much later, Polycarp wrote to Philippi he mentioned πρεσβύτεροι and διάκονοι, but not ἐπίσκοποι. It is, however, perhaps more likely that the two words denote financial officers—the officials perhaps of the poor fund, from which a contribution had been sent to relieve the apostle (Phil. 2:25; 4:10-20).[16] It is true that P. H. Menoud argues that in a brief epistolary greeting Paul would not have spared two words for one financial reference, and that the ἐπίσκοποι are to be thought

[15] *Op. cit.*, pp. 75-76.

[16] The argument is no *e silentio*. The absence of the world πρεσβύτερος could not *prove* that the Pauline churches had no elders, nor could the fact that Paul never describes the appointment of church officials *prove* that no such formal appointments took place (though there is a strong presumption to that effect). Paul's references to leaders take the form of an appeal for recognition of a ministry that has already proved itself in spontaneous service, Christian character, and effectiveness (cf. E. Schweitzer, *op. cit.*, §7k, and note 387). This observation corresponds with the Pauline doctrine of the Spirit.

of as teachers;[17] but we do not know how the funds were administered at Philippi, and if Paul had no reason to mention any other group in addition to the saints as a whole, he would doubtless feel that he had room enough for the two relevant titles.

I have mentioned Menoud's opinion here partly in order to follow him to one further passage, Gal. 6:6, which appears to refer to paid, or at least rewarded, teachers. The interpretation of the passage is disputed,[18] but it probably refers to the same sort of person as is described in I Cor. 12:28 under the word διδάσκαλος. The opening verses of the chapter have emphasized the common pastoral responsibility of all Christians (Gal. 6:1), and their mutual as well as their individual obligations (6:2, 5). There is, however (δέ), a special case: *κοινωνείτω ὁ κατηχούμενος τὸν λόγον τῷ κατηχοῦντι ἐν πᾶσιν ἀγαθοῖς* (vs. 6). The learner has a special duty to his teacher. This should be regarded as a special case of the principle stated as a dominical ordinance in I Cor. 9:14: *ὁ κύριος διέταξεν τοῖς τὸ εὐαγγέλιον καταγγέλλουσιν ἐκ τοῦ εὐαγγελίου ζῆν.*

We must look back over this Pauline material that we may be ready to take a further step. The Pauline conception of the Church is full of "ministry" in the general sense of the term; the Church is Christ's body, and every member of the body has its own *πρᾶξις* (Rom. 12:4); diverse *χαρίσματα, διακονίαι, ἐνεργήματα* (I Cor. 12:4 ff.) are operative. All these activities are functions of the eschatological situation of the new community and bear witness to its possession of the Spirit, in itself the mark of its position "between the times," in the accepted hour, God's day of salvation (II Cor. 6:2). The fact that there is much evidence in Paul of a ministry of the word, of a *διακονία* of loving service to the needy, and some evidence that some Christians are outstanding in the service they render to the saints, but no evidence of an organized hierarchical ministry, is theologically significant. The Church's ministry at large, like the ministry

[17] *L'Église et les Ministères* (Cahiers théologiques de l'actualité protestante 22; Neuchâtel and Paris, 1949), p. 45.

[18] See H. Schlier, *Der Brief an die Galater* (Kritisch-exegetischer Kommentar über das Neue Testament, 10th ed.; Göttingen, 1949), *ad loc.*

of the apostles in particular, belongs to the category of *event*.[19] It is not a function of continuous history but of the unique moment of divine activity. The primary object of all this ministerial activity is witness.[20] The word of the community, which is the primary form of witness, and its deed, which is essential though secondary, point to God's love for men in Jesus Christ and the work he has done on their behalf. What is more, they are actually part of this divine event. This Paul stated most plainly of his own apostolic sufferings in Col. 1:24: *χαίρω ἐν τοῖς παθήμασιν ὑπὲρ ὑμῶν, καὶ ἀνταναπληρῶ τὰ ὑστερήματα τῶν θλίψεων τοῦ Χριστοῦ ἐν τῇ σαρκί μου ὑπὲρ τοῦ σώματος αὐτοῦ, ὅ ἐστιν ἡ ἐκκλησία*. Paul went on to say, *ἧς* [that is, of the Church] *ἐγενόμην ἐγὼ διάκονος*. Since the Church has other *διάκονοι* (in the primary sense) we may suppose that this sharing in the afflictions of Christ is the lot of all Christians, and this, in fact, is stated, or implied, elsewhere. The same point is made from another angle in Rom. 10:14, where there is a plain inference that Christ himself is heard in the word of his preachers. The spread of the gospel and the growth of the Church are themselves part of the eschatological event.

Paul himself was aware of attempts to exalt the ministry, or rather particular ministers, attempts which, because they disregarded this point, reduced what they sought to magnify. It is from this point of view that we should consider his treatment of the false apostles in II Cor. 10-13. There is a large and complicated problem here, and I must be content to pick out one or two special features. Unlike Paul, whose apostleship was marked rather by suffering and shameful treatment than by any visible marks of distinction and success, his adversaries appealed to visible signs to legitimize their ministry. It is true that Paul could often appeal to the same signs and privileges if he wished, but it was very seldom, and only for a special purpose, that he allowed himself to do so. They were Hebrews, Israelites, of the seed of Abraham. They were good speakers. Their ministry had universal recogni-

[19] Cf. J. L. Leuba, *L'institution et l'évenément* (Neuchâtel and Paris, 1950).
[20] Cf. Karl Barth, *Church Dogmatics*, IV, iii, 2, especially pp. 610-14.

tion, and this was acknowledged by the fact that the churches contributed to their support. Thus encouraged, they behaved arrogantly in the churches in which they ministered. They had visions and received revelations. When Paul chose to be a fool he could match their claims, but when he was himself he boasted only of his weakness, in which the invisible power of Christ, secretly anticipating the age to come, was made known. It was they, not he, who illustrated the Jewish *shaliaḥ* pattern, and represented Jewish traditionalism and authoritarianism on Christian soil.

The importance of this for our subject is admirably brought out by E. Käsemann:

> If we may understand the Corinthian intruders on the basis of this Jewish model, their whole appearance, both the openness of their opposition to Paul and the juridical tone of their indictment, gain color. As apostles, they are at the same time inspectors commissioned by the primitive Jerusalem community, which felt itself to be the legal heir of the Jewish central body and of its claims to the authentic transmission and interpretation of the sacred tradition. And on this basis the Corinthian conflict appears as the collision of two concepts of ministry (*Amtsauffassungen*) on the soil of primitive Christianity.[21]

The Pauline letters were written in the fifties and sixties. We must traverse approximately a generation before we encounter the next great burst of Christian writing, in the eighties and nineties. It is not surprising that it differs in several ways from Paul, not least in the picture it offers of the ministry. The Pauline churches were young; they were dominated by their experience of the Spirit of God; they looked for a speedy consummation of their hopes in the Lord's return. The apostle himself was at hand to drive away false doctrines. They felt little need of any other permanent leadership. A generation later the situation was changed. The apostle himself was gone, and this meant both that a new protection against heresy was called for and that the hope of an eschatological consummation within the first Christian generation was shattered. There was a growing awareness that the Church has a stake in the

[21] "Die Legitimität des Apostels," in *Z.N.W.* 41 (1942), p. 57 (p. 37 of the reprint: Darmstadt, 1956).

past, its own past, as well as in the future. We must now consider what the Church made of this new situation, so far as it affected the ministry. We must begin by considering the question analytically, looking at the different blocks of Christian literature that belong to the period.

Some take us very little beyond the Pauline position. This is true, for example, of Hebrews, an epistle which certainly belongs to the second generation, for the author distinguishes himself and his readers from those who heard the Lord (2:3). The apostles had passed on, though they were not forgotten. The Church of Hebrews has perhaps a rather more clearly defined class of leaders than the Pauline churches had. In the last chapter the ἡγούμενοι of the Church are mentioned three times (13:7, 17, 24). The last of these references is no more than a greeting. From the others we learn (1) that the ἡγούμενοι speak the word of God; (2) that their faith provides an example for imitation; and (3) that other Christians should be obedient to them, since they keep vigilant watch over men's souls. These leaders thus combine in themselves the three kinds of ministerial activity which earlier we saw to be fundamental in Paul's thought. It is, however, right to add that Hebrews, which has by no means lost the eschatological outlook, also assumes that all Christians will perform ministerial activity. All are to provoke one another to love and good works (10:24); all are responsible for the drooping hands and the weak knees of their brethren (12:12), and this common Christian responsibility is described by the word ἐπισκοπεῖν (12:15: ἐπισκοποῦντες μή τις ὑστερῶν ἀπὸ τῆς χάριτος τοῦ θεοῦ). The whole church should exercise oversight, and the whole church is rebuked because its members still need teaching when they ought to be ready to teach others (5:12). Hebrews takes us to nothing more explicit than that "capacity for leadership" which "is indicated by readiness to serve." [22]

First Peter also marks no great advance. It is doubtful whether the epistle even mentions presbyters in the technical sense. The word πρεσβύτερος occurs at 5:1 and may refer to "elders"; there are how-

[22] Manson, *The Church's Ministry*, p. 55.

ever two good reasons for supposing that it should be rendered "older men." (1) In 5:5 we meet a second group, consisting of νεώτεροι, who are introduced by the word ὁμοίως: ὁμοίως, νεώτεροι, ὑποτάγητε πρεσβυτέροις. There was certainly no order of "younger men," and the fact that πρεσβυτέροις in the Greek does not have the article suggests that the sense is: You younger men should pay due respect to those who are your seniors. (2) In 5:1 the author describes himself as συμπρεσβύτερος. This is difficult on any view of the authorship of the epistle, unless we may suppose that the reference is to age rather than to a particular ministerial office.

We cannot read out of 4:11 (εἴ τις διακονεῖ) a specific reference to deacons. We should however note in this verse a clear statement of the two basic forms of Christian service: "whoever speaks . . . whoever renders service." The witness is borne in word and deed. The epistle insists, as all parts of the New Testament do, on the universality and mutuality of Christian service. After the reference to older and younger men—who naturally must express their Christian obedience in different ways—the author adds, "Clothe yourselves, all of you, with humility toward one another" (5:5, cf. 3:8).

It makes no great difference whether we take πρεισβύτερος in First Peter to refer to an office or not. Undoubtedly the presbyterate was developing at the time when First Peter was written, and it probably did develop out of the older end of each congregation, notwithstanding the fact that some old men can be very silly and that occasionally you find an old head on young shoulders. Again, "readiness to serve" is the qualification or condition of leadership (ἑκουσίως, 5.2).

Jas. 5:14 has a clear reference to the πρεσβύτεροι τῆς ἐκκλησίας, which again is interesting, though in a minor way. The elders are to be sent for in case of illness; we may compare here Baba Bathra 116*a*: "If anyone has a sick man in his house, let him go to a teacher (*ḥakam*), that he may seek mercy for him." The elders, in fact (whatever the origin of the Epistle of James may be), correspond closely to Jewish officials; we should not have been surprised if James had used here the word he uses in 2:2 and had spoken of the elders of the "synagogue" (assembly). It is worth adding to this that James did not suppose that elders occupy all the ministry of the Church. After saying that elders should be sent for in case of illness, he went on, ἐξομολογεῖσθε οὖν ἀλλήλοις τὰς ἁμαρτίας καὶ προσεύχεσθε ὑπὲρ ἀλλήλων, ὅπως ἰαθῆτε (vs. 16*a*).

With Hebrews, First Peter, and James all too briefly dealt with, we must turn to three divisions of the New Testament that are of outstanding importance in this, as in other respects.

Of these, the first is the Johannine literature, which contains the most profound treatment in the New Testament of the twin problems of eschatology and Gnosticism. Neither in the gospel nor in the epistles is there any attempt to ascribe administrative authority to the apostles, and there is little that bears directly and positively on the development of the ministry, at least as far as its outward ordering and organization are concerned. Indeed, so far as "ministers" appear in the epistles they do so in no very favorable light. It is likely that those who "went out from us," though they were never really "of us" (I John 2:19; 4:1-6), were, or would have liked to be, leading members of the Christian society, perhaps therefore (if the word in this sense is not anachronistic) ministers. They are false ministers, however, because they do not maintain the truth of the apostolic gospel of Jesus Christ, God's Son come in the flesh. In the third epistle (III John 9) we meet ὁ φιλοπρωτεύων Διοτρέφης, in whom some have seen the prototype of the monarchical bishop. This may or may not be true; the important thing is that, bishop or not, he excludes himself from the Christian ministry rightly understood by his flouting of the plain word of Christ. He should have sought to be not first but last of all (Mark 9:35; cf. 10:42 ff.) He contrasts unfavorably with the household of Stephanas, who appointed themselves for service (I Cor. 16:15). Whatever his hierarchical status, Diotrephes is a false witness because he does not love.

From these negative points we may return to the positive contribution to our subject made by the Johannine literature. The emphasis of the Johannine books upon the theme of witnessing has often been remarked and is of central importance. The opening paragraph of the first epistle (I John 1:1-4) is not without grammatical obscurity, but its substance could not be plainer. The writer's purpose is to announce the eternal life that was manifested in and through the historic person, Jesus Christ. In the communication of this message are communion with God and perfect joy. This testimony is the primary work of the apostles—*ὑμεῖς μαρτυρεῖτε, ὅτι ἀπ' ἀρχῆς μετ' ἐμοῦ ἐστε* (John 15:27). By this apostolic word the Church lives, and it is the touchstone of discipleship: *ἐὰν ὑμεῖς μείνητε ἐν τῷ λόγῳ τῷ ἐμῷ, ἀληθῶς μαθηταί μού ἐστε* (8:31).

At the same time there is another mark of Christian ministry in the love that stoops to the menial task of feet washing, and even to the giving of life itself: *ἐν τούτῳ γνώσονται πάντες ὅτι ἐμοὶ μαθηταί ἐστε, ἐὰν ἀγάπην ἔχητε ἐν ἀλλήλοις* (13:35).

There is nothing new in this command, nor in the idea of witnessing. If we ask what is new in the Johannine material, two points—so closely related that they might almost be described as one—may be made.

1. John suggests how the testimony of the apostles came, in the new generation, to be at once the testimony of the whole Church and of the individual witness. With little space at my disposal I cannot do better than quote E. C. Hoskyns:

> In the perspective of the Johannine writings, the first person plural means primarily the original disciples of Jesus, and . . . it is precisely this plural that is capable of expansion to a general "we" and of contraction to a particular "ego." This expansion and contraction is, however, possible only within the sphere of those who, though belonging to a later generation, have been so completely created by apostolic witness and formed by apostolic obedience that they are veritably carried across into the company of the original disciples of Jesus and invested with the authority of their mission.[23]

2. Though the apostles bear witness (15:27, quoted above),

[23] Hoskyns, *The Fourth Gospel,* edited by F. N. Davey (London: Faber & Faber, Ltd., 1947), pp. 100-101.

for John the primary witness is the Holy Spirit who continues his work in the Church until the return of Christ. Here we may turn back to 15:26 (*ἐκεῖνος [ὁ παράκλητος] μαρτυρήσει περὶ ἐμοῦ*), and refer also (among other passages) to I John 5:7, *τὸ πνεῦμά ἐστιν τὸ μαρτυροῦν*. It is because the Spirit is always present that a continuing human witness, and thus a continuing human ministry, is possible.

There is a close kinship between the Johannine writings and the Lucan. In the latter also the apostles are primarily witnesses (e.g., Acts 1:8), and their witness, or word, is that which creates the Church. This is true not only of the word spoken by apostles but also of the activity of humbler evangelists (e.g., Acts 11:19-20). As in John, behind this apostolic testimony, given in the first instance by the eyewitnesses but also by other *ὑπηρέται τοῦ λόγου* (Luke 1:2), lies the testimony of the Holy Spirit himself: *ἡμεῖς ἐσμεν μάρτυρες τῶν ῥημάτων τούτων, καὶ τὸ πνεῦμα τὸ ἅγιον ὃ ἔδωκεν ὁ θεὸς τοῖς πειθαρχοῦσιν αὐτῷ* (Acts 5:32).

Luke thus joins John in setting forth the gospel, committed originally to the apostles but not as their exclusive property, as the creative life of the Church and the staple feature of its witness to the world. Equally, though in a different way, he stresses the importance of the Church's witness through practical love, for it may fairly be said that two of the great turning points—(perhaps the two greatest turning points—in his narrative depend on this theme. The Hellenist movement, originating with Stephen and issuing in the foundation of the mixed church at Antioch and the Gentile mission, began with the appointment of seven men to supervise the already existing administration of charity to the poor. Similarly Paul's last visit to Jerusalem, the outcome of which was his journey to Rome, was motivated by the desire to bring alms to the poor (cf. also Acts 11:27-30). Acts, further, shows us a Church where there is always someone to assume responsibility and render service—that is, in the Christian sense, to exercise leadership.

Indeed, Acts is full of ministers of one kind and another, and it is impossible here to list them and to discuss all the problems which their names and descriptions raise. In Acts the πρεσβύτεροι come into their own. It is even stated in 14:23 that on the return stretch of their first missionary journey Paul and Barnabas appointed πρεσβύτεροι for the churches. In view of the silence of the epistles this can hardly be accepted as historical; if it is we must understand the work of the πρεσβύτεροι in terms of what is said in the epistles about those who preside.[24]

If Luke slips at Acts 14:23, he is probably right when he speaks of elders in the church at Jerusalem (11:30; 15:2, 4, 6, 22, 23; 16:4; 21:18). It is likely that the church in Jerusalem, conscious of being now the true Israel of God, should organize itself on the same lines as the old Israel which it was supplanting, and the Jerusalem elders resemble to some extent the Jewish council.

The picture given in Acts 20 of the elders in the church at Ephesus is somewhat different, and recalls the pastoral epistles. These πρεσβύτεροι, unlike those in Jerusalem, are also described as ἐπίσκοποι (20:28), and it is their responsibility to shepherd God's flock. There can be little doubt that in Paul's speech to these men Luke is holding up to the ministers of his own day what he regards as the true ideal of ministry. It is their duty to continue the work of proclamation, testimony, and teaching that Paul himself has carried out, both publicly and privately (20:20-21, 24, 27, 31). The work of preaching is supported by works of charity, the principle being expressed here in a word of Jesus unrecorded in the gospels: μακάριόν ἐστιν μᾶλλον διδόναι ἢ λαμβάνειν (20:35).

I do not think it profitable here to discuss the appointment of the Seven (Acts 6), since Luke appears to regard them as an *ad hoc* institution; it will be noted that he does not call them deacons.[25] I must also pass over his use of the words "prophet," "teacher," and "evangelist." Luke's main theological service to the idea of ministry, like John's, lies beneath rather than on the surface. He is the Christian historian, and his theological contribution to the

[24] That is, they would be outstanding servants of the Church, recognized as such by their brethren; similarly the elders of Acts 20.

[25] At 21:8 he calls them "The Seven," corresponding to "The Twelve."

New Testament is to be found in his perception that there was and would continue to be Christian history to record. It was, he saw, possible to hold fast to the essentials of Christian eschatology and at the same time to trace the story of a Christian community evolving through the generations within the framework of space and time. It was part of this process that a continuous ministry, not simply a product of the unique circumstances of the last generation of this age, should come into being within the Church. That which gives continuity to the ministry is the Holy Spirit; Luke has no reference to any apostolic or ministerial succession—an astounding omission on the part of the first Christian historian if such a succession is, in fact, essential to the life of the Church. But it is the Holy Spirit who makes men ἐπίσκοποι in God's flock (20:28), and the Holy Spirit is always *there,* and not to be confined within any particular channel. In fact, and to put the matter positively, it is Luke's reinterpretation of eschatology in terms of the Holy Spirit so as to include a serious and significant history of the new people of God that leads him to his view of the ministry, which continues the apostolic mission by preaching the apostolic gospel and reproducing the apostolic witness in word and deed.

As early as the Muratorian Canon[26] it was recognized that the pastoral epistles, though having the form of personal letters, were properly used in *ordinationem ecclesiasticae disciplinae.* No other part of the New Testament deals so explicitly with church order, and the epistles will thus provide a suitable stopping place for our sketch of the ministry in the New Testament.

Two points may be very briefly mentioned, for they would command very widespread agreement. (1) The epistles were not written by Paul. This means that their historical setting is fictitious, and we cannot build a historical reconstruction upon the picture of Timothy and Titus they provide. Even if we could we should be obliged to observe that Timothy and Titus were not irreplace-

[26] See for example B. F. Westcott, *A General Survey of the History of the Canon of the New Testament* (7th ed.); London, 1896, pp. 535, 546.

able "apostolic delegates"—cf. Tit. 3:12.[27] (2) Though the Pastorals show us a more developed situation than any other part of the New Testament, even here ministerial terminology is fluid. That the words ἐπίσκοπος and πρεσβύτερος are applied to the same persons is a widely held and, I believe, correct view. Moreover, Timothy can be described as a διάκονος, and both he and Paul have a διακονία (I Tim. 1:12; 4:6; II Tim. 4:5). διάκονος is not an exclusively technical term.

What the Pastorals understand by the ministry is best seen by considering the nature and function of the Church, the "pillar and bulwark of the truth" (I Tim. 3:15). This does not mean that the truth (or gospel) is dependent on the Church, but that the Church exists to serve it. What the Church is is made clear in II Tim. 2:19. It rests upon a firm foundation which bears a twofold inscription: "The Lord knows his own" and "Let every one who names the name of the Lord depart from evil." The Church is God's elect community called through the gospel, and since every member of it must avoid evil, it must exercise discipline. The Christian gospel and Christian discipline—these are the business of the Church, and it looks primarily to its ministers to supply and apply them.

The Pastorals say nothing about the duties of ministers in relation to the sacraments; they stress repeatedly the central importance of preaching in the minister's task (see, for example, I Tim. 4:11, 13, 15-16; 6:2, 17; II Tim. 2:2, 14-15, 25; 4:1-2, 5; Tit. 2:1, 7, 15). The minister must teach by example as well as by precept (I Tim. 4:12; Tit. 2:7) and must take steps to hand on to others the message he has himself received (II Tim. 2:2). He is equipped and enabled for his work by a special "gift" that accompanies the laying on of hands (I Tim. 4:14; II Tim. 1:6). Ministers receive pay-

[27] It might be argued that though the picture of Timothy and Titus is fictitious, the fictitious picture itself bears witness to the existence, at the time when it was drawn, of "apostolic delegates"—diocesan bishops, or metropolitans, whose authority covered a considerable area. There is some substance in this view, but it misreads the picture. Timothy and Titus are still (in the fiction as presumably in fact) travelling missionaries. See Manson, *The Church's Ministry*, pp. 60-64; Von Campenhausen, *op. cit.*, p. 117; Schweitzer, *op. cit.*, note 321.

ment (I Tim. 5:17), though this does not necessarily mean that they have no employment at all in addition to their ministry.

Ministers also preside over the church (I Tim. 3:4-5; 5:17), exercising the necessary discipline, even to the extent of excluding heretics and troublemakers from the church (I Tim. 1:3; II Tim. 2:15; Tit. 1:13; 3:10-11).

The work of ministers—and for that matter the lives of all Christians—are made more difficult by the context in which they are set. They live in the latter age of human history in which error and wickedness multiply (I Tim. 4:1 ff.; II Tim. 3:1-5; 4:3-4). Their task lies in a difficult and discouraging time; their encouragement is that their work is God's work and that, even though they may be bound, his word is not (II Tim. 2:9).

I have in this chapter given a good deal of attention to the trees, and it is time now to stand back and take a quick look at the wood. It seems to me that our investigations justify the conviction that the New Testament reveals a constant conception of the service of God which is rendered in and through the life of his people. It splits into two parts: A service in word, and a service in action. Men serve God and each other by hearing and believing his word, and then in turn proclaiming it that others may hear and believe it. Each of the verbs I have used—hear, believe, proclaim—is to be understood in a wide sense. "Hear" includes obey; "believe" includes understand; proclaim includes teach and explain. There is no accident in this concentration upon the word; it is a theological concentration and arises out of the fact that God himself has spoken —indeed, has sent to men his personal Word, his own Son.

He who was and is the Word of God spoke to his disciples and gave them the word. He also served them in love, giving his life as a ransom for them, and this service in love also became a part of their ministry—theological in its origin, though absolutely practical in its execution. These are the fundamental forms of Christian ministry which appear throughout the New Testament.

These are the two basic forms of Christian ministry, and we have seen how in the Pauline churches they were distributed in a great variety of individual gifts through the whole membership of the community. We have seen also, emerging alongside them, a third dimension of ministry, in which some members of the Church were moved and equipped to carry to a higher level or over a wider field gifts which were by no means their exclusive property. Sometimes, and naturally, the first and most experienced converts exercised this additional gift of holding the whole community together through their firmer grasp on the gospel and more whole-hearted dedication to the labor of love. Here are the roots of "the ministry" as we know it, but there is still no clear differentiation. The circumstances did not call for organization; the very lack of it was eloquent testimony to the eschatological situation of the Church, which was witnessing the last moments of transition from this age to the age to come, whose word was still Christ's word, whose love was his love, whose suffering was his suffering. The ministry, such as it was, had no purpose but to point away from itself to Christ and to make clear the eschatological event of which it was itself part. I do not wish to suggest that the Church in Paul's day was perfect, but something like this appears to have been the apostle's ideal for it.

Time went on and the eschatological perspective changed till, by the end of the century, it had become much what it is today. It would be as wrong to decry the Church of this period as to idealize that of Paul's age, but it is at least clear where its temptation lay. The Church was settling down in the world; it had a considerable past behind it, and who could tell how long a future before it? Many of its leaders were good men, well aware of their twofold duty in word and service. Others, however, not without thought of their own advantage, helped the Church in the process of settling down by accommodating the gospel to the current Gnostic speculation and their behavior to the standards set by the world. All this can be clearly seen from evidence inside and outside the New Testament.

The situation was taken firmly in hand by the author of the Pastorals; less explicitly by Luke and John. Quite plain moral demands must be laid upon ministers; they apply to all Christians, but if the ministry fails here the body is stabbed in the heart. There was, however, a theological task to achieve as well as a moral one. It is not for the ministry to help the Church to settle down in this age; its calling is precisely the reverse. It must have an eye for the past, for its message—and the Church's life—are rooted in the life, death, and resurrection of Jesus. It must not, however, handle the past as an heirloom, as the rabbis handled their traditions. The Christian witness fails if it does not make clear that now and always the Church lives in the last times; that Jesus Christ, who came but yesterday and will come tomorrow, is always our contemporary; that through the Spirit we live forever in the accepted time, the day of salvation. The ministry is one of God's means of reminding us that we cannot settle down in the traditions we draw from the past and the plans we make for the future, that we are strangers and pilgrims and seek a city out of sight.

It remains only to pick up the thread left loose at the beginning of this chapter. The changing pattern and pressure of eschatology affected the development of the ministry—as of other Christian themes and institutions—not in one way but in two. On the one hand, as time continued and the *parousia* of Christ was deferred the ministry came to be regarded as continuous and successive in an organizational, and authoritative in an administrative, sense. At its best it developed along this line into a tradition-bearing agency; at its worst it became the anchor by which the Church attached itself to this world and the screen by which it protected itself from the urgent immediacy of the present God. On the other hand, where the New Testament theologians found a means of retaining the urgency of primitive eschatology in the continuity of Church history the ministry appears, more or less clearly, as an agent of this eschatological present, rooted in the Word, created by the Spirit, and pointing away from human institutions to the Son of man.

4

The Doctrine of the Church at the Reformation

E. GORDON RUPP

A Roman Catholic scholar has recently protested against reading the historical pronouncements of the Church as a fundamentalist reads the Bible. Rather, he insists, we must begin with the historical setting, of what men were reacting against as well as what they seem to affirm. This may sound a truism, but, as he shows, the results are startling when applied to the Council of Trent, and I suggest they would be equally shaking if applied to the doctrinal section of the Methodist Deed of Union. It suggests the method for this chapter, for in fact we might treat it in several ways. We might adopt the method of many ecumenical confrontations and examine the matter confessionally—giving most of the space to Luther and Calvin—saying less about Zwingli and Bucer, throwing in a few references to Anabaptists out of deference to the recent incursion of the Pentecostalists. More rewarding, we might treat the whole thing in terms of biblical exegesis and see what the Reformers make of the great biblical texts about the Church. To do this would require a large volume to which we might add a further volume on the Reformer's use of Augustine and the old Fathers as exegetic aids. Or we might systematically list some themes and see what the Reformers say about them, but this begs two questions, that there is, in fact, a common ecclesiology of the Reformers, and whether our themes and our questions are, in fact, what might concern the men of the sixteenth century.

To begin with, the historical and empirical context seems justified by the literature on the subject. It has often been pointed out how few are the medieval writings of the nature of the Church. The most fruitful are the discussions about simony, embedded in the very practical Church-state controversy about investitures in the tenth and eleventh centuries. It is surely of great significance that the two principal tracts on the theme "De Ecclesia" are by John Wycliffe and John Huss, those "Reformers before the Reformation," and a work by Torquemada in the fifteenth century which has direct reference to issues raised by heresies. This theme has never been fruitfully studied in a vacuum, but the church has been prodded into it by an existential crisis in its life. Nor is the context alone important. We must always remember the background of the Roman Church of the later Middle Ages—the intricate, formidable overorganized institution with its great administrative departments and its vast civil service, legalized and secularized and degraded to an extent which the Catholic historian Lortz considers would have affronted the conscience of the early church. It is against this institution with its extreme clericalism only that we can understand the theme which I shall dodge, the "Basingstoke" word of modern anticlericalism—the "priesthood of all believers."

I spoke of Wycliffe and Huss as "Reformers before the Reformation," an old-fashioned phrase, against which in my time I too have had my say. As I grow older, however, I find all those old-fashioned platitudes to have something in them, more perhaps than in the bright half truths which have taken their place. And though John Wycliffe has taken a severe mauling in recent years, notably at Oxford (which has by tradition a curious love-hate relation with its evangelical offspring), the new picture of him as a soured, ambitious intellectual will not quite do either. It is becoming increasingly clear (and a comparison of his teaching with E. H. Tavard's "Holy Writ and Holy Church" confirms it) that in his appeal to the authority of Scripture alone he really does point forward. If his Augustinianism has much in common with Bradwardine and Holcot and Fitz Ralph, at least, unlike theirs, and like the Reformers, his was of an explosive kind. He too blew something up. If we ask why Wycliffe's effect was muffled and stultified, perhaps the answer is not just in the intricacy of his scholasticism—but that he lacked what they had, the tool of printing and the megaphone and microphone of humanism, the revival of the sacred languages and a new orientation of biblical theology.

Because Wycliffe and Huss too faced the conflict with Rome, because they too accepted the supreme authority of the Bible and were steeped in Augustine, they naturally said many things which were said later by the Reformers. What they said is more important than the intriguing question of who borrowed what from whom. S. Harrison Thomson has rightly protested against the view that John Huss simply copied out John Wycliffe on the Church.[1] It is evident that the Bohemian church struggle made Huss use Wycliffe much as Tyndale later handled Luther. In the main points of his doctrine of the Church, however, he does follow Wycliffe. There is the same preference—and it is worth thinking about—for the biblical image of the Church, not so much as the Body but as the Bride of Christ, the same definition of the Church as the company "universitas," almost university of the predestined. Huss even follows Wycliffe in his too subtle distinction between Christ's twofold headship of the Church, one external in his divinity and the other internal in his humanity—a distinction which sounds more like the degree regulations of London University than the New Testament! Martin Schmidt has written a long essay on Wycliffe's doc-

[1] Huss, John, *Tractatus de Ecclesia,* edited by S. H. Thomson (Boulder, Colo.: University of Colorado, 1956), pp. viii-x.

trine of the Church in the *Gedenkschrift fur Werner Elert.*[2] Like much of Schmidt's work it deserves to be read with careful attention and with caution, but he stresses the importance for Wycliffe of Christology, of the Church as the counterpart of the poor, humble Christ, and he notes too his strong ethical emphasis and his tendency to rest rather in the law than in the gospel.

Luther did not read Huss until well after the public Church struggle began. His own teaching developed difficulties as a result of the situation in which he was plunged in 1517 and especially when, in the months before and after the Leipzig Disputation of 1519, he studied Church history and the nature of the papal power. A generation ago, in a classic essay, Karl Holl affirmed that the whole of the later Lutheran doctrine of the Church is to be found even before this in his first massive course of lectures on the Psalms (1513-14). This view has been critically examined recently in a luminous essay by Holsten Fagerberg in the Elert volume already mentioned. He concludes that if there is more of a remnant of Catholic doctrine in these lectures than Holl admitted, there is also much here that remained constant and evangelical in Luther's later teaching. Some of Luther's most important later writings are concerned with the nature of the Church, the Schmalkaldic Articles of 1537, "Of Councils and the Church" (1539), *Wider Hans Worst* (1541).[3] In this connection it is worth remembering Erikson's fine image that the papacy is for Luther what the great white whale in *Moby Dick* is to Captain Ahab.

Much as Luther owed to Augustine (an essay by Ernst Kinder in the Elert volume shows how deep and intimate the relation was at this point [4]) his great polarity of the Word and of faith broke through previous and medieval conceptions. The counterpoise is evident in his stress on the *cummunio sanctorum,* the inwardness of the Church, as against the overinstitutionalized Catholicism of his day. It is of great importance that he thinks of the Church

[2] 1955, pp. 72-104.
[3] These will appear in vol. 41 of the new American edition.
[4] Pp. 24-43. See Works of Martin Luther.

primarily as a communion of saints, as an affair of persons, even though we agree with Fagerberg that we must not in a nineteenth-century German way say that Luther's thought is of a *Personen-gemeinschaft.* There is a close connection between justification by faith and the doctrine of the Church. Here, *Coram Deo,* and in our incorporation within the righteousness of God revealed in Christ, all distinctions are done away; there is neither layman nor cleric, but all are one, and all outward distinctions of office are mere *larvae,* masks. I cannot here try to show how important for Luther's view of the Church are his conceptions of earthly authority and the calling of Christians in this world, his view of the whole of human life as set within the providential care of God for all his children, not only his Christian children.

When we turn to the cities of Switzerland and South Germany we find another emphasis. Bernd Moeller has recently suggested some of the ways in which the corporate life of these communities may have influenced the thought of the Reformers.[5] We who rightly insist on demythologizing the patriarchal authority of the monarchical episcopate as it developed in the second century must be prepared to do the same for the Presbyterian view and ask how far the more democratic setup in the cities, and the humanist respect for classic parallels, has affected the Swiss interpretation of the New Testament itself. A more mystical view of the church, perhaps due to that conflation of the modern devotion with German mysticism, which is a feature of much fifteenth-century piety of which John Staupitz was but one expression, is to be found in John Oecolampadius, the most learned patristic scholar among the Reformers. For him it is of the essence of the church that it is a union of hearts in the invisible world. The great Protestant disputation at Berne in 1528 offered as one of its attractions, public preachments by half a dozen eminent Reformers, and on this occasion it is typical that Oecolampadius should take as his theme, "Of the Love of Christ for His Church." When we put side by side what William Pauck says of Martin Bucer and what Martin Schmidt says about John

[5] *Reichstadt and Reformation* (1959).

Wycliffe there are some striking but possibly accidental resemblances. Bucer too begins with a doctrine of election and predestination, Christocentrically conceived. He has a similar ethical interest, the same tendency to legalism. Yet more than any other Reformer, Bucer was at home in Ephesians and Colossians. He had as Strohl says, "a charisma for assimilation," and though he owed much to either Swiss or South German Reformers, there is a good deal in him too of the early Luther.

Oscar Farner in his great work on Zwingli has suggested that Zwingli's doctrine of the Church changed under the impact of his controversy with the Anabaptists in 1528. In his earlier exposition of the "67 articles" and his "True and false religion" he stressed the presence of Christ in his Church as head; and Jacques Courvoisier has lately stressed that this real presence of Christ in and with his whole church is a most important framework, too often ignored, in his Eucharistic doctrine.[6] The doctrine of predestination and election was an important weapon against the Anabaptists, for it cut back behind their debate on the importance of personal conviction, personal experience, and saving faith. Zwingli also has a firm stress on the visible church—which he significantly defined as that of the *kilch horers*—those who are under the word and are under its discipline. In his massive, exhaustive, and rather exhausting biography of Balthasar Hubmaier, Torsten Bergsten shows that Hubmaier kept close to Zwingli in his doctrine of the Church, and was therefore nearer to the Reformers (much as the English Puritan John Tombes is not a Baptist but an Anglican who practiced only adult baptism) than to the Swiss Brethren or the South Germans or the Anabaptists of St. Gall.[7]

The Anabaptists are the great new, exciting field of Reformation studies. There are now masses of new evidence available yet to be assimilated. Franklin Littell in his *Anabaptist View of the Church* properly demanded a retrial of the Anabaptist case.[8] He

[6] *Zwingliana* (1960), vol. XI.
[7] *Balthasar Hubmaier* (1961).
[8] Boston: Beacon Press, 1958.

argued with the engaging brashness of a veritable Perry Mason come to judgment and with rather more bold freedom since his Hamilton Burger and Lieutenant Tragg, in the persons of Melanchthon and Bullinger, have been dead for four centuries. Yet there is some evidence on the other side not to be dismissed as irrelevant and immaterial, and the case presented by Bender and the Mennonite historians is too exuberant not to be modified. Yet we may admit to be proved that it is the doctrine of the Church that lies at the heart of the Anabaptist view in its doctrine of the fall of the church and of hope of the restitution of the Church, in its attitude toward the magistrates and the state; in its opposition to the mixed Church, the *Volkskirche,* or the Established church, there is an anticipation of the Puritan doctrine of the "gathered" church and of the antagonism to the establishment of modern free churches. There is much more to John Calvin than a charisma for assimilation, though it is important that he belonged to a second generation of reformers and that he had important things to say, when we recover from the prejudice caused by the fact that too many Presbyterians treat the Reformation story as summed up in the great watchword *Soli Calvino gloria.* If we sometimes feel that all the interesting things in Calvin have been better said either by Martin Luther before him or by Karl Barth after him, there is still much at which to marvel and admire. No other Reformer has treated the visible Church, which is our mother, with more grandeur or written more solemnly of the ministry and its calling. Those Methodists who are always insisting that ours is a presbyterian view of church polity invariably reveal themselves as holding a much lower view of church and ministry than Calvin's majestic view of the ministerial order and its calling and its place within God's providential order for his Church.

The Anglican divines also belong to the second generation, so that it is remarkable to what extent John Bradford, John Jewell, and Richard Hooker—and even Whitgift—echo the teachings of the Reformers. Obviously then, we cannot simply lump all the Reformers together. Very important are the differences of setting, of time, of emphasis. Rather riskily we can pick out some common notions.

About the question posed by Robert Barnes in 1531, "What the Church is and who be thereof?" there is wide range of agreement. Indeed we might remember that Thomas Aquinas also spoke of the Church as "a congregation of believers" and that the conception of the number of the elect is an integral part of the doctrine of the Mystical Body. But Calvin and Hooker are as insistent as Luther on the inwardness of the Church. "Because a small and contemptible number lieth hid under a huge multitude and a few grains of wheat are covered with a heap of chaff, to God only is to be left the knowledge of his Church, the foundation whereof is his secret election." Hooker said, "The Church of Christ can be but one . . . neither can that one be sensibly discerned by any man, only unto God are they clear and manifest." This does not reduce the Church to a mere notion, however; this is no ecclesiological docetism. "That I have taken the Church to be a spiritual assembly," said Luther, "you have insultingly taken to mean that I would build a church as Plato builds a state that never was."

In perhaps the most important single essay on Luther's doctrine of the Church, Kattenbusch expounded this double element, visible-invisible in Luther's teaching. Quite recently Ernst Kinder in an essay in the *Festgabe fur Joseph Lortz*[9] has shown that in fact Luther used the expression "invisible" seldom and with obvious reserve, that he preferred the expression "hidden" (*abscondita, verborgen*). This hiddenness has a Christological root. As the glory of Christ was hidden in his earthly ministry, so is the Church veiled in infirmities, weakness, and shame. Because of this, its true nature is recognizable only to the eye of faith (*sola fide, perceptibilis*), as we might say, only faith can see that this Cinderella in her rags is *Coram Deo* a bride adorned for her husband. Ernst Rietschel uses the illustration of music, which to a tone deaf person is an unintelligible jumble of sounds, but to one with a musical ear is a coherent melody. "I believe one holy Christian church," said

[9] 1958, I, 173-92.

Luther in 1530, "and so no reason can perceive it, not if everybody were to put on spectacles, for faith is of those things which are not seen." In *Wider Hans Worst* there is the fine sentence: "O it is a high, deep hidden thing is the Church which nobody may perceive and see but only grasp in faith in baptism word and sacrament." This is partly also because human existence is a battle school of faith. "This love of Christ and fellowship with his saints must be hidden, invisible spiritual . . . for were this known to all as earthly communities are known we should not be strengthened and trained thereby to put our trust in the invisible and eternal."

There are remarkable coincidences with this teaching in the English martyr John Bradford. Bradford was the Dietrich Bonhoeffer of the English Reformation, and all that has been saved of his theology are fragments, meditations, and interviews in prison under sentence of death.[10] He was the pupil of Martin Bucer at Cambridge, and he may have been the first eminent English Calvinist. Here are some sentences from his interrogations:

Bp. West:	Who can see your church?
Bradford:	Those, sir, who have spiritual eyes wherewith they might have discerned Christ's visible presence here on earth. Visible indeed is the Church, but men's blindness is great.
Bp. Heath:	You always judge the church.
Bradford:	No my lord, as Christ's sheep discern Christ's voice so they discern the church, but do not judge her.
Dr. Harpsfield:	Tell me whether the Church is visible or no?
Bradford:	Yes, but none otherwise visible than Christ was on earth. We must put on such eyes as good men put on to know Christ when he walked on earth; look therefore as Christ was invisibly known to be Christ when he was on earth; so is the Church known.

Of definitions of the Church, the loveliest is that of Luther in the Schmalkaldic article (1537): "Thank God, a child of seven knows what the church is, the holy believers and the sheep who hear their shepherd's voice." The same polarity of the Word and of

[10] Parker Society, 2 vols.

faith is to be found in the noble first thesis of the Berne colloquy of 1528: "The Holy Christian Church whose only head is Jesus Christ is born out of the Word of God, and forever abides in that Word nor will it hear the voice of strangers. . . ." In 1530 the famous definition of Augsburg (article vi), that the Church is the congregation of believers where the gospel is purely taught and the sacraments rightly administered, tended to influence all later definitions. Interesting, therefore, is the definition in the curious "Dialogue between a father and his stubborn son" translated by the English exile William Roye but which has recently been shown to have been the early Strassburg catechism of Wolfgang Capito:

Son: What manner of a church is this?

Father: It is a company gathered or assembled together of the true and faithful Christian people which are members of one head by the operation of the Holy Ghost and are fastened in one head, Jesus Christ their Lord.

Dr. E. Payne once asked me if this is the first appearance in English of the phrase "gathered church," but it is perhaps that it simply translates the word "ecclesia."

The Augsburg Confession set out the two great dimensions of the Church, Word, and sacraments. Through Luther the Word became one of the magisterial, still unexhausted conceptions of the Reformation. It marks the living presence of God with his people, that presence of Christ in the Church ruling and directing it which Luther early emphasized against the papal claims, and of which John Jewell affirmed, "We need no man to have the whole superiority in the church—for that Christ is ever present to assist his church and needeth not any man to supply his room." God's Word uses the preaching of the gospel as well as the vehicle of the written scriptures. In the first years of the Reformation the doctrine of Word and Spirit were kept close, but the rift between left and right deepened at this point; first the doctrines of an outer and inner Word fell apart, and then the division hardened into an emphasis on pure doctrine, on the one hand (a recent essay by

Lauri Haikola has shown this element to be prominent in Melanchthon's view of the Church), and an increasingly subjective stress on the inner Word, on the other. Nor did the appeal to Scripture mean that the tradition was ignored. In a famous sermon Luther called the Apostle's Creed his "little Bible." The appeal to the old Fathers was an important legacy from Erasmian humanism, and here a turning point may have been the debate with the Anabaptists, or the decision at Berne in 1528 that the notaries in the great colloquy should register only arguments taken from the Bible.

I cannot begin to expound the doctrine of the sacraments from Luther's fundamental insistence on the religion of Incarnation, as always mediated to sinful men by signs, or the spiritualism of the Swiss Reformers and the Anabaptists. All the Reformers insisted that Scripture contained sufficient truth for salvation, but on the scope of Scripture there was an important difference between Reformers and radicals, between those who found in the Bible a blueprint for church order and those who felt that ecclesiastical polity lay within the realm of Christian liberty wherein the Church has authority. Cranmer, in his perceptive letter to the Council in 1552 protesting against the Black Rubric, saw the difference here to be fundamental. The doctrine that we may only do what is explicitly commanded in Scripture he declared to be the very root of the sectaries. Hooker was true to Cranmer when he declared, "Sundry things may be lawfully done in the church so they be not against the Scriptures although no Scripture doth command them, but the church only following the light of reason may judge them to be in discretion meet."

Word, sacraments—then emerged a third dimension, "the discipline of Christ." There was a problem here. If the true church be inward, known only to God, how can fellowship and discipline between Christians be possible?

The problem was solved by a kind of theological gimmick. In his "Bondage of the Will" (1525) Luther distinguished between the rule of faith and the rule of love. "I call the saints the church of God, not by the rule of faith, but by the rule of love. For love is eager to believe the best and hopeth all things . . . and calls a baptized person one of the saints." Bucer extended this thought when he said that by an act of charity we might presume those to be of the Church "who were baptized, who professed the Christian faith, and who walked in godliness." This thought was taken up again by Calvin. "Because the certainty of faith was not necessary, God hath put in place thereof a certain judgment of charity whereby we should acknowledge for members of the church those that with confession of faith and with example of life and with partaking of the sacraments do profess the same God and Christ with us." Zwingli's view of a Christian commonwealth as a prophetic community led him to entrust large powers of discipline to the godly magistrate. His friend Oecolampadius was aware of the dangers of this, and in his great oration to the Basel Synod 1529 he put forward a blueprint for Christian discipline in which laymen and clergy joined together in exercising pastoral care. This was extended by Bucer with a wider use of the power of these lay churchwardens, while his contacts with the Anabaptists led him to experiment with smaller Christian cells, fellowships which did not very long endure. Calvin carried the development of church discipline to a further stage though it is noteworthy that he does not in the Institutes—as does the Scots Confession—reckon the administration of the discipline of Christ as a third dimension to be added to Word and sacrament. Word and sacrament remain paramount for him.

Here was a great dividing line between the Reformers and the radicals. While the Reformers generally accepted the Augustinian view of the visible church as a mixed body in which tares grow along with the wheat, the Anabaptists attempted to frame a pure, gathered church in which a strict discipline was exercised over the godly.

Franklin Littell has stressed the importance for the Anabaptists of a notion of the fall of the Church, of the corruption of primitive Christianity. But of necessity all the Reformers held that corruption had entered the Church. They differed in their pin-pointing of it. Those two extremists Sebastian Franck and his friend Campanus, who in the long march of the Church militant down the centuries regarded themselves as the only two in step, put the degeneration very early, in the title of Campanus' now lost tract "Against all the world from the time of the Apostles." On the eve of the Reformation Lucas of Prague put the fall in the time of Pope Sylvester. Thomas Müntzer drew from Hegesippus in Eusebius a strange doctrine of a fall at the end of the sub-apostolic age. Others, like George Witzel, put it as late as the fifth, sixth, or even the eighth or ninth centuries. It was not only the radicals who consciously sought to regain the primitive Church, however. It was the marrow of John Jewell's apology to insist that "we have returned again unto the primitive church of the ancient fathers and apostles . . . the very head springs and foundations of the church." "We are the true, primitive church," said Luther again and again, "and the old former church shines forth again now as the sun from the clouds behind which it was shining all the time but not clearly." Richard Hooker said: "They ask us where our Church did lurk? In what cave of the earth it slept for so many hundreds of years together before the birth of Martin Luther? As if we were of the opinion that Luther did erect a new church of Christ. No, the Church of Christ which was from the beginning, is, and continueth unto the end."

The Reformers pressed home the consequences of viewing the Church as the New Israel. In the pamphlet dogfight between Karl Stadt and John Eck in 1519 there is an interesting and revealing aside in which Eck said that properly speaking the Church cannot repent and cannot sin, for it is the Body of Christ. The Reformers treated the sin of the New Israel more ruthlessly and in the same language with which the prophets had arraigned the old. They really faced the question of what happens when the New Israel also rebels, denies, disobeys, forsakes, and what shall be done in the end thereof? "I put the case," said John Jewell, "what if an idol be set up in the Church of God?" Then he added, "What if some thief or pirate invade and possess Noah's Ark?" That is a striking figure, Noah's Ark flying the skull and crossbones, the

Jolly Roger. Here is a great matter for the Reformers, the battle between the two cities, the elect and the reprobate, the true and the false church, which do not simply co-exist, but are in tension and conflict in a dynamism which runs through the whole of church history and gives it an apocalyptic character. This is what the forthright Scots Confession calls "the Kirk Malignant"—it is a thing requisite that the true Kirk be discerned from the filthy synagogue, the horrible harlot, "the Kirk Malignant." The Reformers did not generally completely unchurch Rome or utterly equate the false church with the papacy. Luther drew on Augustine's doctrine of the two cities going back to Cain and Abel. Other Reformers drew on the book of Daniel for an interpretation of Christian history. Vadianus of St. Gall, in a kind of Toynbee-like study of human history, distinguished four ages of the Church. Martin Bucer similarly discussed the "times of the Church" in his *De Regno Christ;* while John Foxe in England and Glaccius Ullyricus in the *Magdeburg Centuries* saw history as the rise and fall of anti-Christ. Yet there is no ultimate dualism here, no pessimism, for there is the thought of the victorious presence of the risen Lord of the Church at God's right hand, who has shed forth the Spirit and who shall come again. Thus the doctrine of the Word emphasizes the leadership of God, the creative newness within the Israel of God leading his people into new truths, new insights, new deeds. Luther said:

> Even if it were the highest novelty, since it is the Word who is giving orders, what matters is not the novelty but the majesty of the Word. For what I ask is not new that faith does. Was it not a new thing when the apostolic ministry was instituted? Was it not new when Abraham offered his son? Was it not new when Israel crossed the Red Sea? Will it not be a new thing when I pass from death to life? But in all these things it is not the newness but the Word of God which counts.

I daresay much of this chapter must seem irrelevant to many of you to the plight of Methodism and the ecumenical situation. I rather hope so. Church history has nothing to teach us if we rush into it with our own questions and ask things about which we are concerned, but which were not so important in a past age. Only when we sit down first and listen to the men of the past talking among themselves, minding their own business; listen to their questions; glimpse a little of their proportions; do we find that, after all, there are some clues, some things written for our examples.

One day in the last century, two old men sat together on a park bench in the city of Birmingham. The one was a Methodist supernumerary (I have the story from his grandson). The other was John Henry Cardinal Newman. They talked about what the church is and who be thereof. Newman took the other's umbrella and poked in the dust a circle on the ground and said, "I think you have to get the circumference right." The old Methodist took his umbrella back and poked a single hole in the center and said, "Ah, we think that you must begin with the center, and if you get that right the circumference will look after itself." Well, it is an apocryphal and perhaps implausible tale but it may have a truth about Protestantism, and perhaps about Methodism too. It may be that the Church is more like a ray of light than a box with tidy edges. I suspect that every ecclesiology at some point blurs those edges, that eschatology interrupts every attempt to define and guard the Christian circumference. The Reformers were surely right in returning to the center, of beginning *Coram Deo,* with God who is revealed in the Incarnate Son, hidden in his humiliation and suffering but risen and exalted—and hidden after another fashion until the appearance of his glory. When John Knox was dying his wife asked him what passage she should read to him from Holy Scripture. "You know," he said, "the place where my soul first cast its anchor." She turned to John 17, to the theme of Christ's priestly office, his intercession for his Church and for his world. In the end, more fundamental than the question, What is the Church and who be thereof? is the theme "Of the Love of Christ for His Church." Somewhere there too the ecumenical movement must learn to cast the anchor of its hope.

5

Baptism and the Family of God

ROBERT E. CUSHMAN

Present-day Confusion

The promptness with which baptism in the name of Jesus[1] assumed a central place in the worship of the primitive Church is a historical fact that the average Protestant Christian today is, I fear, about equally unprepared to take in or, unhappily, to trouble himself about. It seems evident that for hosts of Protestant people —both lay and clerical, at least in the American churches—baptism survives as a solemn but nearly unintelligible rite persisting by the inertia of unassailable, because immemorial, tradition. Excluding the Baptists—for whom "believer's baptism" is ordinarily the visible sign of grace unto repentance on the one hand and public profession of faith on the other—evangelical churchmen as I know them scarcely conceal mild embarrassment in their practice of adult

[1] See Acts 2:38; 19:5; I Cor. 1:13. Cf. W.F. Flemington, *The New Testament Doctrine of Baptism* (London: Society for Promoting Christian Knowledge, 1948), p. 38.

as well as infant baptism and fumble conspicuously when pressed for a coherent rationale of the sacrament as such.

Whatever their notion of baptism in the economy of adult salvation, a good many Methodist ministers covertly if not openly adopt the view that infant baptism signifies only a kind of dedication. An unusually candid if theologically naïve instance is provided us in a very recent issue of *The Christian Advocate* (U. S. A.) by the Reverend Harrison R. Thompson of Pomona, California.[2] In Thompson's view there is no impoverishment of infant baptism in regarding it as "dedication" of the child to God on the part of committed parents. He insists, however, that the parents must be faithful and "active" church members, devoted to the proper nurture of the child. Such a view, he thinks, is constructive and avoids all the imponderables respecting the child's capacity for faith or receptivity of regenerating grace. In point of fact, Thompson sees baptism primarily from the side of the nurture offered by the community and hardly at all from that of the divine gracious activity.

Thompson's disregard of God's gracious act in baptism is corrected by F. Ernest Stoeffler in a companion article of the same issue.[3] He supports the tradition of infant baptism by appeal to the views of John Wesley, which he finds significantly reflected in *A Treatise on Baptism* published by Wesley in 1756, a work commonly regarded as a dependent revision of one published by Wesley's father, Samuel, in 1700.[4] Stoeffler argues that John Wesley's views on infant baptism must be seen as lying within the tradition of Puritan "covenant theology," an important feature of which is that children of Christian parents are quite as truly inheritors of the new covenant as were Hebrew children inheritors of the old. As circumcision was a sign and seal of the inclusion of the children of the old covenant, so baptism is the appropriate sign and initia-

[2] "Infant Baptism: Dedication" (May 24, 1962), vol. IV, no. 11, pp. 11-12.

[3] "Infant Baptism: Entry into Covenant," pp. 10-11.

[4] *Vide A Treatise on Baptism* in *Works,* London, 1830, Third Edit., X, 188 f. For the provenance of this document and likely dependence upon Samuel Wesley's *A Short Discourse of Baptism,* 1700, see *Proceedings of the Wesley Historical Society,* edited by W. F. Swift (June, 1960), XXXII, pp. 121-24.

tory rite for the inheritors of the new.[5] Stoeffler urges renewed consideration for the view that by baptism the child becomes part of the new Israel and is ingrafted as a member into the Body of Christ. He thinks he sees the indication that Wesley believed that on attaining the age of discretion the youth "must consciously assume the conditions of the covenant." [6] Thus the objective grace that began its work in infant baptism fulfills its work in conversion and commitment of riper years. Regeneration is a process, and Stoeffler thus believes he finds the basis for Wesley's insistence upon the "new birth" over and beyond the grace of infant baptism.

Whether Stoeffler's thesis can in fact be vindicated depends upon more careful marshalling and assessment of a mass of evidence than his short article permitted or than can be achieved in this chapter. The available documents plainly show that Wesley retained infant baptism in the economy of redemption. In the *Treatise on Baptism* he reproduced his father's assertion that baptism is "the washing away the guilt of original sin" and that, therefore, infants "are proper subjects of baptism." [7] In both the *Treatise* and *Thoughts upon Infant Baptism* baptism is, indeed, seen to be the Christian analogue to circumcision, whereby the individual is admitted to or inherits the new covenant, but there is, perhaps, insufficient evidence that Wesley shows direct dependence upon the elaborate covenantal theology of such representative Puritan divines as John Owen[8] or William Strong.[9] On the contrary, one has the impression that the covenantal theory is embraced within a composite of catholic ingredients of wider provenance.

Adverting again to the present-day uncertainty in Methodism regarding the meaning and role of the sacrament of baptism, it

[5] Cf. J. Wesley, *Thoughts upon Infant-Baptism Extracted from a Late Writer*, Bristol, 1751. This document, which is a brief summation of W. Wall's *The History of Infant Baptism*, does indeed set forth the covenantal viewpoint in this form and provides ample basis for Wesley's expressed notion of infant baptism as "the circumcision of Christ," the sign of the new covenant.

[6] *Op. cit.*, p. 11.

[7] *Works*, X, 190, 193.

[8] *The True Nature of a Gospel Church* (London: 1689), pp. 3, 7.

[9] *A Discourse of the Two Covenants* (London: 1678), chap. IV.

is obviously attributable to many historical factors. In America it is first of all attributable to theological indifference that has greatly prevailed among churchmen during the present century. To this must be added the fact that Methodism of the advancing nineteenth-century American frontier was fervently evangelistic, soundly practical, complacently moralistic, and innocent, if not contemptuous, of niceties of ecclesiological doctrine. A third factor is the triumph, in various forms, of the anthropocentric and basically Pelagian theology of the Enlightenment during the nineteenth century. Fourthly, one must refer to large elements of uncertainty and, perhaps, ambiguity in the express utterances as well as exasperating silences of John Wesley himself regarding the meaning of baptism and its significance—especially in relation to the implications of the Revival for the conception of both church and sacrament. To my knowledge this obscurity was not really much clarified by Wesley's theological succession, even by Richard Watson. In the fifth place, it is probably necessary to say, in the light of two hundred years of scientific biblical scholarship, that the problem of baptism faced by Protestantism today is attributable to the manifest uncertainty surrounding the genesis of Christian baptism as it suddenly takes its assured place in the Christian cultus during the transition period between the earthly ministry of Jesus and the post-Pentecostal emergence of the Church and its worship. In this chapter I propose to consider only the two final and, apparently, remotely related factors. We shall look first to the Wesleyan tradition regarding the sacrament.

Wesley on Baptism

Eric Gallagher, in a series of articles in *The Irish Christian Advocate,* entitled "The Methodist Doctrine of Baptism," [10] has reviewed Wesley's writings on the subject and concurs with W. F. Flemington in the general view that, while Wesley never renounced "baptismal regeneration," and on occasions assumed it, yet his explicit teaching that the grace of baptism could be and was fre-

[10] August 4-25, 1950.

quently lost introduced ambiguity regarding the nature and role of the sacrament for succeeding Methodist people.

If one attends Wesley's direct utterances—especially the sermons "Marks of the New Birth" and "The New Birth"—he finds a number of points plainly asserted: (1) First, that baptism and the "new birth" are not one and the same thing. (2) Second, that in the doctrine of the Church of England baptism is not identified with the new birth. (3) Third, that baptism is an outward sign that signifies but is "distinct from regeneration, the thing signified." (4) Fourth, nevertheless, the "church supposes that all who are baptized in their infancy, are at the same time born again; and that it is allowed that the whole office for the baptism of infants proceeds upon this supposition" even though the manner of God's work escapes us. (5) Fifth, that baptism is to be understood as "the circumcision of Christ," but that, once baptized, one is not necessarily now a child of God.[11] (6) And finally, that the plain empirical fact is that apart from "new birth" and its marks in sanctification of life, baptized or unbaptized, men remain children of the devil and will perish everlastingly.

For Wesley the mark of the new birth from above is holiness, the renewed image of God in man; namely, as he wrote in "Marks of the New Birth," "the whole mind that was in Christ Jesus." It is the "birth from above," he said in "The New Birth," *"figured out by baptism,* which is the beginning of that total regeneration without which no man shall see the Lord." (Italics mine.) In Wesley's sermon at Oxford in 1733 on "Circumcision of the Heart" he said "that the distinguishing mark of a true follower of Christ, of one who is in a state of acceptance with God, is not *outward circumcision, or baptism,* or any other outward form, but a right state of soul, a mind and spirit renewed after the image of Him that created it. . . ." (Italics mine.)

What, then, is so far apparent is that baptism may be the instrument of washing away of original sin and forgiveness of the same

[11] In the *Treatise on Baptism,* regeneration is not only expressly affirmed but the baptized is "grafted into the body of Christ's Church." *Works,* X, 192.

in the case of infants, yet it does not constitute more than a beginning of the process of regeneration, which requires the "new birth" and sanctification to complete. The forgiveness of original sin does not exclude the likelihood of actual sin, and as Wesley encountered actual men, including himself, in their actual bondage to sin, he found the way of release to be the new birth—"true, living, Christian faith"; namely, "a sure trust and confidence in God, that through the merits of Christ his sins are forgiven, and he reconciled to the favour of God." [12]

The crux of the matter seems to be that from personal experience and clear-eyed observation Wesley, the realist, recognized that, however valid baptismal regeneration was, sin nevertheless reigned, even though it was also true that God remained.

Furthermore, the experience of the Revival induced Wesley somewhat to subordinate sacramental grace in baptism to the moment of converting or justifying grace, with two consequences: First, to accent more emphatically the difference between the cleansing grace of infant baptism and the justifying grace of conversion and assurance, or "new birth"—a distinction, however, that had been explicit with Wesley since 1733. Second, and derivatively, to make a sharper distinction between the "new birth" of the adult Christian, the thing signified, and the baptismal rite; that is, the sign. Whereas Wesley in the *Treatise on Baptism* could speak of it as "the ordinary instrument of our justification," to which God hath tied us but not tied himself, his sermonic utterances increasingly disclosed a tendency sharply to distinguish form and substance, the *sign* and the *reality*. The reality is the "new birth" which, seemingly, tends to become loosely associated with its sign, indeed almost to the point of dissociation. For the clear distinction he made between sign and thing signified Wesley found full authority in both Westminster and Anglican "catechisms." The sign is juxtaposed to the thing signified as an "external" contrasted with an "internal" change wrought by God in the soul. The clinching empirical fact of the Revival was that Wesley witnessed case

[12] "Awake Thou That Sleepest."

after case of such internal change independent of and antecedent to the baptismal rite. On the other hand, he saw gross, even if baptized, sinners inwardly transformed.

All this does not mean that Wesley felt called upon, as in fact he never did, to deny the regenerative efficacy of infant baptism. On the contrary, he felt himself called upon to assert only the plain fact that the baptized often lived as if unregenerate and that the question was not whether baptized persons, as he put it, had once received the Holy Spirit, but whether they were *now,* in point of fact, temples of it. In sum, whatever may be the efficacy of baptism for voiding original sin, experience proved that baptism, as the sign, was not regularly—certainly not in the case of children—effectual for bringing forth the thing signified. It might be, and Wesley evidently believed it was, the beginning of the regenerative process and, in God's sovereign mercy, an effectual means of grace; but evidently Wesley also early believed that without "the circumcision of the heart" or the "new birth," the regenerative process did not have its fulfillment.

In entertaining these positions, however, Wesley was sensible of no incongruity between his own view and that of the "Homily on Prayer and Sacrament," which defined sacrament as "a visible sign of an invisible grace, that is to say, that setteth out to the eyes, and other outward senses, the inward working of God's free mercy, and doth, as it were, seal in our hearts the promises of God." In both the *Treatise* and the *Thoughts upon Infant-Baptism,* baptism is described as the "seal" of the promises of the new covenant in Christ. In the *Treatise,* as edited by Wesley, it is even declared that in baptism "we are regenerated or born again" and made the children of God by adoption, yet the virtue of baptism is not "the outward washing" but "the inward grace." It may, however, be questioned whether Wesley's view is in complete accord with the 25th *Article* on the sacraments wherein it is declared that they "be not only badges, or tokens of Christian men's profession: but rather they be certain *sure* witnesses and *effectual* signs of grace, and God's good will toward us, *by which* he doth work invisibly in us. . . ." [13] Of this Wesley would not deny what is affirmed, but he would, I think, caution against what is implied; namely, that the efficacy of grace in infant baptism suffices unto salvation.

To understand this demurrer we must make reference to Wesley's anthropology and to his pervasive view that grace can be and is resisted and that until it is decisively embraced, or until grace effectually triumphs in the "new birth," the grace of baptism need not and will not be effectual unto salvation. This is most thoroughly spelled out in the sermon "The Spirit of Bondage and Adoption." There Wesley speaks of "the heathen, baptized or unbaptized," signifying thereby that the baptized are heathen still if the love of God is not yet "the ruling principle" of the soul. This position is quite consistent with the statement concerning the efficacy of infant baptism in the *Treatise,* which reads: "Herein a principle of grace is infused, which will not be wholly taken away, *unless we quench* the Holy Spirit of God by long-continued wickedness." (Italics mine.) But Wesley accepted the fact that the "infused" grace of baptism can be and is resisted, and often almost to the point of quenching the Spirit, as in the case of the "natural man" (nearly but not quite asleep to God) who is portrayed in "The Spirit of Bondage and Adoption."

Here, then, it may be, are the reasons why Wesley affirmed, on the one hand, that baptism—by which he principally intended infant baptism—is the outward sign of a real infusion of regenerative grace, while, on the other, he could hold that baptism was regularly not adequate unto salvation. It is adequate in principle but not in fact, because the adult becomes, though not necessarily, resistant to grace and at length must cease to resist.[14] But to cease is not a human act but another effectual work of grace, the grace of justification or the "new birth." Accordingly it appears evident that

[13] Cf. Thomas Rogers, *Doctrine and Religion Professed in the Realm of England* (London: 1629), p. 142. Italics mine.

[14] For a treatment of Wesley's doctrine of freedom as the power to resist grace, see the author's essay "Salvation for All" in *Methodism,* edited by William Anderson (Nashville: The Methodist Publishing House, 1947).

in Wesley's mind the grace of justification and, eventually that of sanctification, does not negate but perfects the grace of baptism.

In the order of God's nurturing and redeeming work, therefore, the grace of baptism comes first and is the "seal" or earnest of further promises under the covenant of Christ. Wesley seems to have held that the further promises—since actual sin actually intervenes—are to be fulfilled in the grace of justification, although it is to be admitted that this is not quite explicitly declared. If this construction is sound, then, in the logic of the matter adult baptism was for Wesley far from a normality and becomes, after justification, something of a superfluity, although permissible. While admittedly Wesley did not clarify these matters, it would be entirely erroneous to suppose that his increasing stress upon justifying grace after 1738 in any way makes void the grace of baptism. Rather, on the whole, it presumes it. While justifying grace tends to depress the role of infant baptism in the economy of salvation, yet it is pervasively plain that Wesley viewed infant baptism as the inaugural influence of grace upon the life of the child, incorporating it within the community of faith and nurture.

The tenor of Wesley's utterances reveals, then, that infant baptism entails a first work of grace, a "means" God himself enjoins by the institution of Christ. As a work of grace it is effectual, but not necessarily or invariably unto salvation. The autobiographical statement in the *Journal* under the famous dateline Wednesday, May 24, 1738, offers Wesley's personal testimony on this point. He wrote: "I believe, till I was about ten years old I had not sinned away that 'washing of the Holy Ghost' which was given me in baptism. . . ." He then proceeded to describe a state of soul quite comparable to that "second" condition of man—in fear of God under the law—set forth in his later sermon "The Spirit of Bondage and Adoption." Thus, we have primary evidence: (1) First, that Wesley affirmed a real efficacy of grace in infant baptism (supported by Christian nurture); (2) second, that a falling off from this grace was experienced in his own youthful years.

Once again, the explanation of this is a practical one; namely, the power of sin or the tendency thereto remaining in the human soul in which God does not yet fully reign. Accordingly "the circumcision of the heart," or "new birth," or justifying grace, must complete what is begun in baptismal regeneration. All this was for Wesley, quite objectively, the work of God, and in virtue of the freedom of man to resist grace, it is just as possible for the grace of baptism to be attenuated or "quenched" as for the justified adult sinner to fall from grace. Neither baptism nor justification, however, is for this reason depreciated. Both display God's search for the sinner, but the Calvinistic doctrine of "perseverance" is rejected or inapplicable save to those sanctified ones of whose identity Wesley disclaimed any knowledge.

Finally, for Wesley, the sacrament of baptism was always a "sign" and never a cause of an invisible grace. Since the connection between "sign" and thing signified is never a necessary one—in virtue both of God's freedom and of human freedom of resistance—the grace of the sacrament is not *ex opere operato,* though it is more nearly so in infant baptism than in adult baptism. Wesley does not doubt that in the sacrament God truly works, yet it is all but certain that Wesley's own mind is represented in the words of the *Treatise on Baptism;* namely, that God has appointed infant baptism as the "ordinary means" of inaugurating human regeneration, but also, that while God has tied us to this means, he has in no wise tied himself. Wesley is regularly opposed to any domestication of sovereign grace, and God's freedom over his grace makes way for its "surprising" manifestations which actually broke forth in the multifarious phenomena of the Revival.

Now, having clarified these issues, we still have to ask of Wesley, what is baptism? Why does it signify the washing away of sin, regeneration, or justification? What is the inherent connection between baptism and the forgiveness of sins? In answer to these questions Wesley is no more helpful than the great tradition in which he stands, and yet the contemporary churchman is pressing for answers to just these questions, and upon adequate answer to them the recovery of the significance of baptism greatly depends.

Baptism of the Elect One

Throughout the history of the Church we may, I think, discern a deep-lying but stubbornly resilient tension, if not contradiction, between the sacraments conceived as "means of grace" and the free working of God of which the sacraments are acknowledged to be "signs" and sentinels. The recurrent problem seems to be that the human mind is prone to exchange the sentinel or sign for the work of God and, being already in command of the sign, by a shift of perspective, comes into assured possession of that work itself. Herein is to be found the perennial temptation of man; namely, to make his salvation manageable, predictable, and within his own hierarchic keeping and reach. To be sure, the phrase "means of grace" may be employed in either of two ways. It may signify God's designated and ordinary way of acting redemptively or, and by a subtle shift of emphasis, it may denote the *organon* man presumes to have in his keeping of doing such things as afford him assured access to the divine favor.

Sacerdotal religion of all varieties takes its rise and flourishes by addiction to the second mode of interpretation. Always it is but a shift of the eye and a sleighting glance of the mind that turns the sacrament from a sentinel, alerting men to the present divine activity, into a sacred agency through which the divine activity is first confidently expected to evince itself and, then, again, is gradually and unobtrusively regarded as induced. The onset of this mentality is always accompanied *pari passu* with the idea of a priestly caste especially qualified to be custodian of the sacred agency. Somewhere, sometime, perhaps in the age of Cyprian, this transformation ripened in the Christian church. With Augustine it was, seemingly, fully established, as indicated in these propositions from Augustine's *Enchiridion:* First, *all* who attain to the grace of baptism die thereby to sin. Second, they are "*thereby* alive by being reborn in the baptismal font. . . . There is no one who does not die to sin in baptism." Third, "infants die to original sin only." Fourth, adults die both to original sin and to additional actual sins. By the time of Augustine baptism had become the assured means of *regeneratio,* as, in Justin Martyr, it was already on the way to becoming so.[15]

Wesley's problem with the sacrament, and perhaps our own, has something to do with this development. Wesley might have seized upon Augustine's distinction between the efficacy of infant baptism as voiding original sin and adult baptism as affording remission of both kinds, original and actual, but there is limited evidence of any such awareness on Wesley's part, and scant evidence of direct or intentional dependency. As for the process by which the sacrament is imperceptibly but decisively transformed from a sign and sentinel of the divine activity into an instrumentality of it so as to confer grace *ex opere operato*—a view which no less an Anglican than Thomas Rogers repudiated as Papistry[16]—we are well advised to turn to the New Testament for criteria of evaluation.

So we come at length to ask the question, what is the meaning and role of baptism as a crucial moment of both life and worship in the primitive Church? In what follows I shall be propounding a thesis, rather irresponsibly, for others to confirm or to refute.

To me it has always been a striking fact that Jesus was baptized but did not himself baptize, John's anachronistic and contradictory testimony notwithstanding.[17] Correspondingly, it is remarkable that the first preaching of the Word by Peter on the Day of Pentecost issues in the exhortation to repent and be baptized in the name of Jesus unto the remission of sins and was followed, on the part of those who received the Word, with prompt compliance. (See Acts 2:38, 41.) Next it seems to me of importance that baptism was expressly "in the name of Jesus" and none other, as Paul insisted. (See I Cor. 1:13. Cf. Acts 2:38; 19:5.) Finally, it is significant that according to the record of Acts baptism in the name of

[15] See Justin Martyr, *First Apology,* 61. In Justin's famous account of baptism it is possible perhaps to see the subtle process by which the *sentinel* of grace is being transformed into the *instrument* of regeneration and illumination. Cf. J. N. D. Kelly, *Early Christian Doctrines* (London: A & C Black, Ltd., 1960), p. 194.

[16] See Rogers, *op. cit.,* p. 146.

[17] *Vide* John 4:1-2. Cf. Flemington, *op. cit,* p. 29.

Jesus, conspicuously in two places, follows upon the impartation of the Holy Spirit—in the case of Paul himself (10:18) and in that of Cornelius and his household (11:47-48). To summarize, why, then, did Jesus not baptize? Why, after his death and resurrection, was baptism for the remission of sins promptly proclaimed? Why was baptism explicitly in his name? And, finally, was baptism the unexceptionable agency of the forgiveness of sins, or was it, in fact, an agency at all?

In answer to the question, why did Jesus not baptize? I venture the proposition that Jesus did not baptize because all that baptism really signified was in process of being summed up, literally epitomized, in his ministry as the Elect One, the true Israel of God, and that until his ministry was perfected in total submission to the Father, further baptisms, like those of John, were neither appropriate nor possible.

To unpack the implications of this proposition, I begin by accepting the tradition of Mark that Jesus did not inaugurate his public ministry until John was delivered up (Mark 1:14). Next, we are to credit the tradition not only that Jesus accepted baptism at the hand of John, but that, in the midst thereof, Jesus became aware of his singular and unique mission and ministry. Further, that his singular election was determined and crystallized *in its distinctive form* by the meaning of the baptism he was undergoing as he apprehended it in a moment of overpowering illumination or revelation. Yet, again, we are to agree with Carl H. Kraeling that the distinguishing circumstances of John's baptism, that singles it out from "all the other ablutionary rites of later Judaism is its eschatological context, its association with a proclamation of the coming day of judgment." [18] Likewise, we are to accept Kraeling's carefully derived conclusion regarding the meaning of John's baptism; namely,

> that the water of baptism represents and symbolizes the fiery torrent of judgment, and that the individual by voluntarily immersing himself in

[18] *John the Baptist* (New York: Charles Scribner's Sons, 1951), pp. 113-14.

the water enacts in advance before God his willing submission to the divine judgment which the river of fire will perform. John's baptism would, therefore, be a rite symbolic of the acceptance of the judgment which he proclaimed." [19]

This provides us with material for the next step. It is this that Jesus understood in one luminous moment, that his election to Sonship was indissolubly united with acceptance of total submission to God's will. Further, that on behalf of wayward Israel he must accept in his own person God's judgment; that is, God's annihilation of all sin. On its negative side, acceptance of judgment entails refinement and suffering; on its positive side, it is entire obedience to the rule of God. Henceforth, as is symbolized in the Wilderness sojourn, the existence of the elect one, the faithful Israel, is existence in temptation. In every case the form of temptation is disposition to claim the prerogatives rather than to accept the heavy responsibilities of election. This was the perennial form of old Israel's temptation to which it recurrently succumbed. H. H. Rowley has shown that Israel's election was election for service.[20] In the Elect One both the election and its attendant temptation are recapitulated to issue, however, in victory over temptation. This is the ministry of Christ issuing in the victory of the cross and the vindication of the resurrection.

Thus, our Lord takes upon himself in his ministry the *peirasmos*, the eschatological tribulation, the judgment of God upon man's rebellious waywardness, and, in "fulfilling all righteousness" in his own life,[21] through entire submission to God and entire service-

[19] *Ibid.*, pp. 117-18. Cf. Cullmann, *Baptism in the New Testament,* translated by J. K. S. Reid (London: Student Christian Movement Press, 1950), p. 10. See also Ethelbert Stauffer, *New Testament Theology,* translated by John Marsh (London: Student Christian Movement Press, 1955), p. 23. "John's Baptism is an eschatological covenant sign. For John is the herald of the imminent universal conflagration."

[20] *The Biblical Doctrine of Election* (London: Lutterworth Press, 1952), pp. 43, 45-46.

[21] Matt. 3:15 may represent a pericope that combines the author's apologetic improvisation with an authentic word of Jesus, though not necessarily in original context.

ability to men, actualizes in his own person the two commandments on which hang all the law and the prophets. In the power of this initial victory over *peirasmos* our Lord enters upon his public ministry with no word of doom, but with the "good news" that the time is fulfilled, the kingdom of God is already at the door, and with the call to repent and believe it, indeed, to receive it. Jesus' initial proclamation presupposes his own private Christology. It is the divine disclosure that his election *is* his own appropriation of the *peirasmos,* the tribulation of the final judgment, or all that is really implicated in baptism as John preached it.

It is because Israel after the flesh did not receive the *euangelion,* although the publicans and the harlots did, that the *peirasmos,* the tribulation of judgment, loomed up as the inescapable prospect and awful destiny of the Elect One. In this context and with this background, we can better comprehend two inexpugnable words of Jesus to his disciples. On the one hand, his word in the Lukan pericope, set in a late context: "Ye are they which have continued with me in my temptations [*peirasmoi*]" (Luke 22:28). It plainly suggests that the vocation of the Elect One was service to God in continuing trial and testing of fidelity to his calling that now must be perfected. Secondly, there is the authentic word, now made perhaps more intelligible, "I have a baptism to be baptized with; and how I am straitened till it be accomplished!" (Luke 12:50.)

W. F. Flemington has properly adjudged a hidden but profound significance in this word he calls "indubitably authentic." [22] He regards it as a veiled allusion to Jesus' death, signifying "the inauguration of that wider 'ministry' to which he looked forward, as surely as his baptism in the Jordan was the prelude to his ministry in Palestine." [23]

This is almost the point, but not quite. The truth seems to be

[22] *Op. cit.,* p. 31. Cf. D. M. Baillie's favorable evaluation of Flemington's thesis in *The Theology of the Sacraments* (New York: Charles Scribner's Sons, 1957), p. 75. Cullmann is to be cited as sharing the general standpoint of Flemington's thesis regarding the authenticity of the Pauline view of baptism as "participation in the Cross of Christ." Cf. *Baptism in the New Testament,* pp. 14-15 *et al.*

[23] *Ibid.,* p. 72.

that Jesus' ministry (*diakonia*) *was* baptism (*baptismos*) or was summed up in it; that is, it was the acceptance of the judgment of God upon sin and, or what is its obverse side, entire obedience to the Father's will. Baptism, thus, became the symbol of all that was overtly expounded in the substance of Jesus' ministry and was consummated in the cross. Baptism is, perhaps, the distinctive form or vehicle of the messianic consciousness of Jesus. But baptism points not directly to the cross but to the ministry which is fulfilled in the cross. If acceptance and obedience entailed rejection and death, then this also was an inherent part of the ministry; that is, part of the vocation of the elect of God. If this is so, we are not far from the conception of the vicarious sacrifice. This added dimension is suggested by the fact that baptism always meant to Jesus death to self-will in preferment of God's will—the subordination of prerogative and privilege to radical obedience in service. His death would, then, mean the last full measure of devotion and self-surrender. In yet a further sense, it is the acceptance of judgment, God's judgment of death upon sin, and through such acceptance Jesus' baptism would be accomplished or perfected.

Several deeply embedded traditions of the gospel account become luminous on this hypothesis. The first is the pericope of Mark 10:35-40 prefaced by the request of the sons of Zebedee for special preferment in the age to come. Jesus' reply indicates that the condition of pre-eminence is capability of sharing "the cup" he was about to drink and "the baptism" he was about to undergo. Here both cup and baptism are evidently paralleled in Jesus' thought. Mark made no other reference to baptism subsequent to his account of Jesus' baptism by John (1:9). Now it reappears, not as a past event but as a present expectation, indeed the present tense indicates it to be a present reality going on to accomplishment, as in Luke 12:50.

Certain deductions are permissible: (1) That the passage is, although an authentic word of Jesus, also a *post eventu* explanation of the two sacraments of the early Christian cultus. (2) That the earliest gospel plainly understands the baptism of Christ to have been a continuing process fulfilled in his death of perfect obedience and, thus, perfecting his ministry. (3) That baptism and ministry are inseparably united so that the meaning of the one illuminates the significance of the other. (4) That the condition of inheriting the privileges of the new age is participation with Christ in his baptism, which is to say, his ministry of perfect obedience. (5) That baptism implies repentance and entire submission to the divine judgment upon sin but also, and positively, perfect obedience. It is entrance into the Kingdom. Thus it entails remission of sins but also points to newness of life as the vocation and destiny of the penitent. (6) Finally, however, the passage suggests that Christian baptism is shaped and determined in its meaning by the positive content with which the ministry of Christ unto death irrevocably embues it. Consequently it must, henceforth, always be "in the name of Jesus" and none other. Both the baptism which John practiced and the rule of God which it heralded were realized in the ministry of Jesus.

In reference to the second tradition to be mentioned, we agree with the views of Carl H. Kraeling that the passages (Mark 9:9-13 and Matt. 11:7-15) are important witnesses to the very great significance which Jesus attached to the person of John the Baptist—"a prophet? yea, I say unto you, and more than a prophet" (Matt. 11:9). This estimation could hardly have been accorded without hesitancy and reserve by the early Church, jealous, as it was, of the supremacy of the Lord Jesus. But it is not only, as both Kraeling and R. Otto agree,[24] that John was for Jesus the divinely authorized herald of the last days; more than that, *in John's baptism there was prefigured for Jesus the essential meaning of the ministry of the elect of God.* It signified the rule of God, the Kingdom, not considered as time and place, but as the fulfillment of the election of Israel—the election which, we may say, Jesus both received and espoused in his baptism. In baptism submission to God's judgment and, *eo ipso,* God's will became the paradigmatic form of

[24] Kraeling, *op. cit.,* p. 145. Cf. Otto, *The Kingdom of God,* etc. (London, 1951), p. 109.

election, and therewith of Jesus' own ministry (*diakonia*). Its rationale is definitely summarized in Luke 22:24-29—cognate with Mark 10:41-45—where supremacy is, paradoxically, equated with uttermost service. Baptism becomes the emblem of election and the symbol of total service or ministry that is to be shared by Jesus' disciples.

Finally, there is the famous *lutron* passage of Mark 10:45 that concludes Jesus' exaltation of *diakonia* and his reply to the sons of Zebedee: "The Son of man came not to be ministered unto, but to minister, and to give his life a ransom for many." Recognizing that dispute over this passage is voluminous, I observe only that, in the fact of rejection by the leaders of Israel, Jesus must view his ministry *as an offering made to God,* since it was not presently appropriated by men. It was an offering the Father had it in his power to use for the ultimate fulfillment of his purpose.

It may be argued that the enpersonalization of worship is what distinguishes Old-Testament from New-Testament service of God. The Old Testament looks forward to sacrifice, not of goats and bulls, but of "a broken and a contrite heart" (Ps. 51:17). Isaiah exhorted his people, "To what purpose is the multitude of your sacrifices unto me? saith the Lord" (1:11). "Wash ye, make you clean; put away the evil of your doings from before mine eyes" (1:16). Jeremiah looked to the day of a "new covenant" when, "saith the Lord, I will put my law in their inward parts, and write it in their hearts" (31:33).

With transcendent and mysterious clarity, we may believe, Jesus saw that baptism means sacrifice, the entire dedication to God, not of any surrogates, but just exactly of the self. How God would use it in his unsearchable wisdom for man's salvation remained hidden in his secret councils, but in the light of man's rebellious waywardness, baptism must come to mean what Jesus did "once, when he offered up himself" (Heb. 7:27). Baptism became, then, the fulfillment—that is, the enpersonalization of worship and, at the same time, the fulfillment of the two great commandments: Thou shalt love the Lord thy God, but so that, in such love, the neighbor is not excluded but embraced. At the least, the *lutron* of Mark 10:45 signifies that, in total commitment to the Father, the largest possible benefit to God's people is assured.

In the foregoing exposition I have offered the reasons why Jesus did not baptize. It was because all that baptism really signified was in agonizing process of being epitomized by realization in Jesus' own ministry as the elect of God. Until his ministry—that is, his baptism—was accomplished it could not properly be offered to others. It had first of all, as the Lukan saying has it, to be accomplished (12:50).

Further, we are now possessed of better explanation as to why baptism in the early Church was promptly and exclusively offered and accepted in Jesus' name. The heart of it is *that John's Baptism had been fulfilled;* that is, actualized and perfected in the ministry of Jesus unto death. Further, death was overthrown in resurrection. Baptism was no longer, therefore, merely perfect obedience unto death; the total submission to the judgment of God upon sin had issued in the overwhelming triumph of the resurrection. For the early Church, then, baptism quickly symbolized the passage to life through the way of perfect obedience unto death. Before long its sign undoubtedly came to be the cross, the symbol of perfect obedience and also of life through death. The sign of the cross in baptism is known to Tertullian, and according to Augustine, baptism and the cross are always conjoined.[25] As baptism signified the way to life through death, it followed that the believer who bore Jesus' name must follow in the same way. In this sense, it may be, the earliest Christians were called followers of *the way.*[26] In this perspective the rationale of baptism and its inseparable connection with the name of Jesus is rather plainly suggested in the exhortation: "Whosoever will come after me, let him deny himself, and take up his cross, and follow me" (Mark 8:34*b*). To do this was to

[25] *Temp. Ser.* 101. *Semper enim cruci baptismus jungitur.*

[26] *Vide* Acts 16:17; 18:26; 19:9, 23. Also John 10:1; 14:4, 6. Justin Martyr still speaks of baptism "in the name of Jesus" but also of the trinitarian formula as if in his own day the latter were superseding the former. *First Apol.,* 6.

accept baptism in Jesus' name, a thing self-evident in the early Church.

While the problem remains complex, it is now more apparent why baptism for remission of sins was promptly proclaimed as the burden of early Christian proclamation. To repent and to be baptized are coimplicates if not surrogates one of the other. To participate with Jesus in his baptism was to identify oneself with his perfect obedience and self-offering to God. This plainly meant to die to sin and, proleptically, to be united to Christ in his victory over both sin and death. Baptism, therefore, quickly becomes the inaugural moment of Christian worship; namely, self-offering to God which, by the same token, carries with it forgiveness of sins. Paul then, in the famous passage (Rom. 6:1-7), simply spells out what was only implied, so far as our records go, in the baptismal rite. One can readily share the view of W. F. Flemington that "what St. Paul has to say about baptism represents no innovation, but rather the filling out of ideas already implicit in primitive Christian teaching." [27]

Now we come to face the final question, Was baptism the unexceptionable agency of the forgiveness of sins, or was it an agency at all? Our problem becomes a good deal more complex. Let us begin with the question of agency. Justin Martyr speaks of "conversion" antecedent to baptism and even refers to baptism as "dedication," presumably of self.[28] Both the "conversion" of Paul and that of Cornelius and his household precede baptism. Plainly, also, this was the observation of Wesley in the ferment of the Revival, and Isaac Ambrose had early taught him the reality of the fact.[29]

Are we not faced with the likelihood that the Holy Spirit, the cleansing and renewing power of God, "bloweth where it listeth" so that none know, as John declared, "whence it cometh, and whither it goeth" and that "so is every one that is born of the

[27] *Op. cit.*, p. 73.
[28] *First Apol.*, 65.
[29] Isaac Ambrose, whose principal works Wesley republished, taught that the "new birth" may through God's Spirit come before, with, and after baptism. Cf. *First Things or the Doctrine of Regeneration* (Glasgow, 1737), pp. 18-19.

Spirit" (3:8)? Evidently, if we are to speak of agency in baptism or apart from it, we always intend the agency of God, and, too, the transformation of existence from alienation to reconciliation, accomplished by God's Spirit, is not restricted to a specified number of *bona fide* vehicles. This seems to be the hard lesson that Peter learned first at Joppa and then at Caesarea, which lesson also suggests that formalization of thought had already gone a long way before he got there. A fundamental, a dialectical tension pervades all Paul's teaching; namely, between "sacrament" and Spirit of Christ.

Nevertheless, there is a sense, perhaps many, in which baptism is agency. In the first place, it is historical agency in that above all it *is* the ministry of Jesus Christ fulfilled in perfect obedience unto death and vindicated in the resurrection from the dead. In it God acted for the establishment of his rulership and for man's salvation. In it, furthermore, God continues to act and, through its distinctive power, recalls the erring and restores them to community with himself.

Secondly, baptism is agency in so far as its reenactment is recapitulation of the saving ministry of Jesus Christ in a personal existence, but recapitulation is not real without the *intercession* of the Holy Spirit. To say that the Spirit is given in baptism is to say that without the Spirit baptism is merely a rite and not a recapitulation of Christ's ministry.

But, thirdly, baptism is agency in the further sense that recurring baptism in the usage of the Church is a continuing proclamation by the Church of the nature and ground of its own existence. The ground and nature of its own existence *is* baptism; that is, the perfected and exalted ministry of Christ. In baptism the Church signifies its intent to incorporate either infants or adults into the ground of its own existence; it embraces the individual within the ministry of Christ, which is its own essence. Nevertheless, it does this only in entire dependency of its life upon Christ and in the power of the Holy Spirit.

In each of the three cases, then, baptism is agency only through the overruling divine activity of the Spirit. In no case, including the case of Jesus' baptism—*i.e.,* his ministry unto death—is baptism agency in the sense that its being or efficacy can be referred simply to its historical form or resident potency. Therefore, it is never possible to say that its reenactment conveys grace; this would be to domesticate grace. It is only possible to say that grace *has been* conferred in baptism or that grace *may be* conferred in baptism—but never that baptism *will* convey grace. Thus, we can say of the first baptism, "grace and truth *came* by Jesus Christ." Of the second, we can say the ministry of Christ *has* been recapitulated in baptism of believers. Thirdly, we can say that the Church *has* exercised its intent to embrace infants or adults within the ground of its existence effectually. We cannot say, however, that baptism in any of the three modes *will*—that is, *ex opere operato*—necessarily manifest such efficacy. In the case of Christ, this would be to affirm that his ministry is reproducible and thus to deny his divinity. In the other cases, it would be to put the keys of the Kingdom within the keeping of the Church. But God is sovereign over his Spirit as well as over his Word.

It follows that baptism is agency when God makes it such. It also follows that baptism was not and is not the unexceptionable agency of the forgiveness of sins. Here, of course, I speak not of baptism of Christ but of baptism in his name. Nevertheless, it remains true that in God's sovereign freedom baptism may be a "means of grace" either to children or to adults. It may be a means of regeneration in so far as, in the showing forth of its essence, in baptism, God makes this expression of the Church's ministry a vehicle of his forgiving and renewing power. Nevertheless, if the Church is conformed to the mind of Christ the agency of the sacrament is not to be "grasped" so that the Church accounts itself on an equality with God (Phil. 2:6). On the contrary, in the sacraments the Church empties itself of all pretense so that through these instrumentalities the Holy Spirit of God may be all in all. When that is so the sacrament may be, in God's freedom, a true sign or sentinel of his regenerating power.

Baptism and the Church

As a fourth division and something of an addendum to this chapter, it is now to be admitted that nothing has been said explicitly about one half of its conjunctive title. My assigned topic was "Baptism and the Family of God." By this somewhat quaint phrase those who composed the title doubtless intended to signify the Church. It is a phrase which had some currency in early seventeenth-century Puritan literature and is actually instanced, to my knowledge, in the writings of William Perkins. Perhaps its peculiar provenance is the "covenant theology" of Witsins, Ames, Perkins, and their successors. Frankly, I have not had opportunity to trace its lineage. The term does not occur in the New Testament so far as I am aware, but supposing it may serve as satisfactory surrogate for the Church, the relation of baptism to the Church can be stated in terms consequential of the foregoing analysis.

If baptism in the primary sense *is* Jesus' own baptism, his ministry of perfect obedience unto death, his vicarious acceptance of God's judgment upon sin, and his glorious resurrection, then, plainly, in this primary sense baptism *was* and *is* constitutive of the Church. Baptism is the condition *sine qua non* of the Church, the new Israel or people of God, and only those who are somehow united to Christ in the fullness of his ministry—that is, his baptism—are constitutive members of his body.

Thus, in the second sense, baptism is recapitulated in the lives of believers but as a derivative and altogether dependent reality, dependent in both of two ways, first, upon the full perfect and sufficient sacrifice of Christ and, second, realized by the inner working of the Holy Spirit. In this second or derived form baptism is extension and perpetuation in time of the ministry of Christ. And this is the visible Church. In this way we might venture to say that in the community of believers so constituted there is realization of the eschatological reality; namely, re-established community 'twixt God and men, or reconciliation. Through baptism, first in the ministry of Christ, then through its recapitulation in the lives of men, the will of God comes to be acknowledged and done on earth as it is in heaven. In this revised form the Church becomes the eschatological community in time.

A caution is always in order, however, in view of the perpetual existence of the Church in temptation—the temptation to transform a divine event into a manageable agency. While the words realization, recapitulation, and participation are, with respect to baptism, decisively important, they cannot be spoken nor their reality anticipated save in deference to the antecedent or prevenient activity of the Holy Spirit. Accordingly, baptism in the derivative sense is always something that, strictly speaking, the Church *observes* or *acknowledges* as done, not something it does. Its temptation is always that of supposing that by being in possession of the "sign" it is *eo ipso* in command of the "reality." For this there is no warrant, as I believe Wesley perceived, and accordingly he veers away from a sacerdotal ecclesiology.

A third consequent respecting baptism is this. Since the meaning of baptism is rendered explicit in the ministry of Christ, baptism replaces forever the sacrifice of "goats and bulls" as the author of Hebrews so clearly understands. The sacrifice of the Temple is superseded and henceforth becomes the wholly enpersonalized sacrifice of "a broken and a contrite heart" open now to larger, and logically if not actually, total obedience. This is justification that looks toward sanctification.

Finally, then, the question presses very hard: not *what* but *when* is baptism? The answer is when God makes it so, and while it might be in the baptism of the infant, preventing grace is, as Wesley divined, not ordinarily so far effectual as that justifying grace is not also a necessity in the process of redemption.

6

Confirmation and the Lay Membership of the Church

HERBERT J. COOK

A

The People of God exists by God's choice, not by man's desire. The claim of the Church of Christ to be the "elect race," therefore, makes entry into the Church an acknowledgment of God's work rather than an expression of man's decision. The outward sign of entry into the Church is baptism, in which the new member is presented and the grace of God claimed and proclaimed for him. The analogy between Christian baptism and the initiation of the People of God in the Old Testament was perceived by Paul, who wrote to the Corinthians:

> You should understand, my brothers, that our ancestors were all under the pillar of cloud, and all of them passed through the Red Sea; and so they all received baptism into the fellowship of Moses in the cloud and sea. . . . And yet, most of them were not accepted by God, for the desert was strewn with their corpses. (I Cor. 10:1-5.) [Scripture quotations in this chapter are from the New English Bible.]

The stress in this passage on the fact that baptism is no guarantee of final acceptance pinpoints the historical analogy to the very beginning of the exodus. Baptism is compared with the moment when God began to lead his people out of Egypt. His call and choice constituted the People of God. The Israelites had not yet become the People of God by conscious decision; that was to happen at Sinai. And not all of them reached Sinai. Paul does not take the analogy as far as this, and we must avoid pressing it too far. It does, however, set forth the difficulty which has been acutely felt in the Church—and more particularly with the practice of infant baptism—that while the sacrament of baptism is a means of the all-sufficient grace of God, it is also insufficient to make a man a participator in the community of grace.

Several passages in the New Testament suggest that this insufficiency was recognized from the beginning, for other rites are mentioned either in connection with or in addition to baptism. In Paul's experience at Damascus the imposition of hands by Ananias preceded his baptism. The purpose of the former action Ananias made clear, "that you may recover your sight, and be filled with the Holy Spirit" (Acts 9:17). Here a widely distributed rite for recovery from sickness was given a further purpose in the gift of the Holy Spirit. Then followed baptism with water. Thus the two essential elements of Christian baptism were present at the baptism of Paul—water and the Spirit. Another occasion on which the gift of the Spirit preceded baptism is Peter's experience at Caesarea. While he was speaking to the household of Cornelius

> the Holy Spirit came upon all who were listening to the message. The believers who had come with Peter, men of Jewish birth, were astonished that the gift of the Holy Spirit should have been poured out even on Gentiles. . . . Then Peter spoke: "Is anyone prepared to withhold the water for baptism from these persons, who have received the Holy Spirit just as we did ourselves?" (Acts 10:44-48.)

In other cases, the gift of the Spirit follows baptism. Peter obviously expected this in Acts 2:38; Paul refers to it in I Cor. 12:13; and the absence of the gift of the Spirit to the Ephesians who had been baptized by Apollos led to the further rite of the laying on of hands, after which the Holy Spirit came upon them (Acts 19:1-7).

In this last case the context suggests that the baptism of the Ephesians is not to be regarded as Christian baptism, but rather the kind of baptism associated with John the Baptist. The second rite of the imposition of hands cannot therefore be maintained as necessary for Christian baptism, or as a necessary sequel to baptism, on the basis of this passage. A more notable instance, however, is found in the mission of Philip to Samaria, which resulted in many being baptized. The apostles in Jerusalem then sent Peter and John to Samaria, who prayed that the converts might receive the gift of the Holy Spirit. "For until then the Spirit had not come upon any of them. They had been baptized into the name of the Lord Jesus, that and nothing more. So Peter and John laid their hands on them and they received the Holy Spirit." (See Acts 8:5-17.) The *monon de,* emphasized in the translation "that and nothing more," clearly suggests that baptism "in the name of the Lord Jesus" is not enough. We are left in doubt, however, where lies the deficiency. Was Philip one of the seven (Acts 6:5) not authorized to confer baptism by the Holy Spirit, but only baptism by water? Was the authority for baptism by the Holy Spirit reserved to the apostles only? Ananias would not be an exception to apostolic imposition of hands, since he was directly commissioned for this office and was thereby virtually an apostle. In the account of the conversion and baptism by Philip of the Ethiopian eunuch the Spirit is mentioned immediately after the baptism, but not as falling on the eunuch, only in snatching away Philip. The Western Text at this point makes an addition to insist that the Spirit did fall on the Ethiopian in connection with his baptism: "The Holy Spirit fell upon the eunuch; and an angel of the Lord snatched away Philip" (Acts 8:39). The interest of this addition is that, although the interpolation may not represent an original text and so the Lukan view, it was nevertheless reasonable for the interpolator to suppose that Philip had the power to confer baptism by the Holy Spirit, and that this authority was not reserved to the apostles only. Dr. Rawlinson would interpret the narrative of Acts 8:5-17 "as betokening the endorsement by the two apostles of the action of Philip in baptizing Samaritans (despite their unorthodoxy from the point of view of strict Judaism), and as setting the seal of divine approval on it." (*Christian Initiation,* pp. 19-20.) G. W. H. Lampe would go further than this and suggest that, in addition to this official endorsement, there is involved something akin to ordination, in the establishment in Samaria of a new nucleus of the missionary Church. The imposition of hands by Ananias has also implications of this sort, since we are told that Saul immediately began to preach. Thus at Samaria and in the conversion of Paul important moments in the development of the Gentile mission are marked by acts of ordination. This is going beyond the evidence, however. The only secure conclusion from the narrative is that the Samaritans who were converted under Philip's preaching were incorporated into the Church by baptism with water and by the coming of the Holy Spirit which followed the imposition of the apostles' hands. In this particular instance two rites appear to have been necessary.

The only other clear link between baptism and the imposition of hands is in Heb. 6:1-2, in a list of the rudiments of Christian teaching. The inclusion of "laying-on-of-hands" suggests that an elementary acquaintance with the Church and its teaching would have introduced anyone to this established and recognized rite.

Although there is a clear connection between the imposition of hands and the baptism of the Holy Spirit, it is not a simple connection. If baptism by the Spirit was always accompanied by the laying on of hands it is difficult to see why the rite should be so often not mentioned. At Caesarea Peter did not lay his hands on Cornelius and his friends; he seems to have been astounded that the Spirit fell upon them. At Pentecost Peter told the converts, "Repent and be baptized, every one of you, in the name of Jesus the Messiah for the forgiveness of your sins; and you will receive the gift of the Holy Spirit" (Acts 2:38). Imposition of hands is not mentioned here, nor in Acts 16. In the many offices which the Spirit gives to the Church, in Paul's various enumerations of these, imposition of hands is not mentioned, but since baptism and the eucharist are also omitted, little weight can be placed on this silence. Where, however, in answer to a request for directions (as in Acts 2:38 and Acts 16) concerning the way of salvation no mention is made of imposition of hands with baptism, the omission is significant. We cannot accordingly conclude that the entry of the believer into the Church in New Testament times *must* be effected by the laying on of hands as well as by baptism.

The second rite mentioned in the New Testament in association with baptism is that of sealing. The epistle to the Ephesians has two references which suggest that the initiation of the Christian included an act of sealing: "And you too, when you had heard the message of the truth, . . . and had believed it, became incorporate in Christ and received the seal of the promised Holy Spirit" (1:13); "And do not grieve the Holy Spirit of God, for that Spirit is the seal with which you were marked for the day of our final liberation" (4:30). John Wesley's sermon on the latter text, "On Grieving the Holy Spirit," points out three ways in which we are sealed by the Holy Spirit:

> 1. By receiving his real stamp upon our souls; by being made the partakers of the divine nature.
> 2. By receiving him as a mark of God's property; as a sign that we belong to Christ. And,
> 3. As an earnest and assurance to our own spirits, that we have a title to eternal happiness.

This exposition follows the usual lines of interpretation, linking the seal of the Spirit with the renewal of the image of God in man and giving it eschatological significance.

In his "Plain Account of Christian Perfection" Wesley interprets the former text. Question 26 reads: "Does St. Paul mean any more by being 'sealed with the Spirit,' than being 'renewed in love'?" The answer is:

> Perhaps in one place, (2 Cor. i.22) he does not mean so much; but in another, (Eph. i.13) he seems to include both the fruit and the witness; and that in a higher degree than we experience even when we are first "renewed in love." God "sealeth us with the Spirit of promise," by giving us "the full assurance of hope;" such a confidence of receiving all the promises of God, as excludes the possibility of doubting; with that Holy Spirit, by universal holiness, stamping the whole image of God on our hearts.

The words "full assurance of hope" are brought in from Heb. 6:11, but their intrusion does not invalidate Wesley's exposition. As he pointed out in the "Notes on the New Testament" on the same text: "The sealing seems to imply, 1. a full impression of the image of God on their souls; 2. a full assurance of receiving all the promises, whether relating to time or eternity."

Wesley's interpretation of both texts, therefore, excludes the idea of sealing as a sacramental sign. Such a sign is suggested by referring to Ezekiel 9, where the man clothed in linen is commanded to mark with a cross the foreheads of the people who are to be saved from destruction. In the book of Revelation, where the same thought is taken up, the mark on the foreheads of the faithful is called the seal of God (7:1-8; 9:4). Paul also may have had Ezekiel in mind when he spoke of being "marked for the day of our final liberation" (Eph. 4:30). It was inevitable that this sign should be compared with circumcision, and in one notable passage Paul brings together baptism, circumcision, and the mark of the Christian:

> God forbid that I should boast of anything but the cross of our Lord Jesus Christ, through which the world is crucified to me and I to the world! Circumcision is nothing; uncircumcision is nothing; the only thing that counts is new creation! . . . In future let no one make trouble for me, for I bear the marks of Jesus branded on my body. (Gal. 6:14-17.)

How figurative this language may be is left to our imagination. It is certainly not to be wondered at that early liturgies of baptism included the rite of consignation, the sign made by the bishop on the forehead of the candidate.

Attempts have been made to trace to the New Testament the Syrian practice of anointing (administered before baptism), which seems to have been given more prominence in initiation than baptism. The passages cited—Gal. 4:6; Rom. 8:15; I Cor. 12:3—support a conclusion that the Spirit may indeed be manifest in a man before baptism, but not that any particular rite was involved.

Yet anointing is associated with baptism, although a specific rite cannot be proved. Paul links anointing with the seal of the Spirit: "And if you and we belong to Christ, guaranteed as his and anointed, it is all God's doing; it is God also who has set his seal upon us, and as a pledge of what is to come has given the Spirit to dwell in our hearts." (II Cor. 1:21-22.) In I John 2:20-27 the anointing is twice mentioned as the source of the Christian's knowledge, the enlightenment imparted by the Spirit. Anointing, from its associations in the Old Testament, suggests royal, priestly, and prophetic offices, and in its application to the Christian would emphasize his being united with Christ the Anointed One. I Pet. 2:9, which especially gathers these offices together in the Church of Christ—a "royal priesthood . . . to proclaim . . ."—does not mention anointing in connection with them. The evidence for anointing as accompanying or following baptism is very slender for the New Testament period, but anointing is so unquestionably scriptural that it is not surprising that the early Church used it as a sacramental rite.

Four rites are thus associated, more or less vaguely, in the New Testament and the period immediately following: Baptism, imposition of hands, consignation, and anointing. It is impossible to maintain that they were all always used, or even that any one other always accompanied baptism. A. J. Mason assumes that the imposition of hands was in the early days of the Church universally practiced. He distinguishes between the activity of the Spirit as the agent *ab extra* of baptismal regeneration and the inward presence of the Spirit mediated by the bishop's hands in confirmation. Confirmation is thus the more important initiatory rite. Dom Gregory Dix contends for an early establishment of confirmation at the hands of a bishop on Apostolic authority. "Confirmation was in the Apostolic

Age regularly administered before Baptism in water . . . the original matter of the rite was a baptism by affusion in oil . . . confirmation originated as the Christian equivalent of the circumcision imposed on proselytes by Judaism. . . ." (Thus was established the Mason-Dix Line in support of the sacrament of confirmation.) The evidence is not clear enough to support these claims, however. There must have been some variety of practice in which the only constant element seems to have been baptism with water, to which was sometimes, or even frequently, added one or more other rites to signify baptism by the Holy Spirit. This does not necessarily mean that baptism with water could not be the full Christian baptism by water and the Spirit. Peter at Pentecost seems to assume that water baptism included the gift of the Holy Spirit, and on other occasions the beginning of the Christian way was simply termed baptism (Acts 16:33; I Cor. 12:13; Col. 2:11-12). Yet the evidence is there that in some cases it was thought necessary to ensure or mark the seal of the Spirit by adding other rites.

B

From this variety of practice uniformity did not emerge, but at least a clear pattern of initiation at length became evident in the early Church.

1. The Catechumenate: the candidate was prepared by instruction, and confessed his faith.
2. Baptism with water.
3. One or more other rites: (a) Chrismation; (b) imposition of hands; (c) consignation, which emphasized or ensured the indwelling of the Holy Spirit, the new Christian's ingrafting into Christ, and the branding of him as Christ's property; all of which could have been assumed as imparted by baptism itself, but by some must have been thought to be attendant on these further rites.
4. The first Holy Communion.

The theological difficulties which might have arisen with any attempt to give clear definition to the significance of the further rites were postponed as long as the whole initiation was one occasion.

Theological significance could still be attached to the whole, in which the parts had dramatic differentiation rather than theological. But the growing practice of infant baptism in the Church demanded a clear assessment of each particular in the rites of initiation.

If a person was to be baptized as soon as possible after birth it was obvious that the Catechumenate and the Holy Communion were inappropriate, so that the unity of the initiation would be broken. The Eastern Orthodox Church preserved the unity of the rite by enlisting the participation of parents where the infant could not respond. Thus baptism followed confession of faith; then the child was anointed (perhaps with consignation included in the rite); and lastly came Holy Communion. The "Apostolic Constitutions" suggest that, while baptism could take place in the bishop's absence, the anointing must await his coming. Where this regulation was observed the initiation must have been divided into two parts, with an interval of time, dependent on the bishop's visit, between them. The unity of the rite was, however, preserved by letting the priest anoint the child with oil blessed by the bishop. While this unity was maintained theological difficulties were not pressing.

In the Western Church infant baptism became limited to the act of baptism with water. On the authority of Acts 8:17-19; 19:6; and Heb. 6:2 the further rites of initiation with the first Holy Communion were postponed to an age of spiritual maturity. It became immediately important to define the significance of this second part of initiation. Did it confer anything which baptism did not? Was it simply a reinforcement of baptism? Did it mark the gift of the Holy Spirit, as in Acts 8? We need not for our purpose attempt an account of the variety of opinion which arose in efforts to deal with these questions. From the confusion of thought of this period the clearest statement appears in Pseudo-Eusebius' Homily on Pentecost:

> The Holy Spirit therefore, who comes down in his health-giving descent upon the waters of baptism, imparts his fulness to give sinlessness;

in confirmation he affords a further accession to give grace. . . . In Baptism we are reborn to life, after Baptism we are strengthened (confirmed) for the fight; in Baptism we are nourished, after Baptism we are fortified.

The word "confirmation" is frequent from the fifth century onward as the name for the second part of initiation, its meaning being explained along the lines suggested in Pseudo-Eusebius. Confusion still persisted, however. The Holy Spirit may be present at baptism in his *fullness* (*plenitudinem*), but it appears that the Christian needs a *further accession* (*augmentum*) of the Spirit. Is this further gift of the Spirit necessary to salvation? The general decision and final pronouncement of the Church was that it was not. But Thomas Aquinas' definition of confirmation tended to leave the question still open: *hoc enim sacramentum est perfectio baptismi,* with the ambiguity of the word *"perfectio."*

C

The reformers in general accepted the practice of confirmation, while rejecting it as a sacrament. The stricter definition of sacrament led to the rejection of the Roman rite, but the obvious need for reinforcement of baptism made some form of confirmation necessary—even if it consisted only of instruction preceding first communion. The practice of anointing was rejected as not being evidenced in the New Testament, whereas imposition of hands was maintained by many, because there was warrant for it in Scripture as well as in the practice handed down through the Church Fathers. There was a general strong insistence on the catechumenate. The instruction and examination of candidates, in which they confessed their faith, were the necessary precursors of whatever other rite was observed in confirmation. The whole rite of initiation was accordingly:

A. Baptism—usually in infancy.

B. Confirmation—years later—consisting of:

  1. Instruction and examination;
  2. Confession of faith with promises;

3. A ceremony, often with imposition of hands, of confirmation by the Holy Spirit;
4. First communion.

The word "confirmation" was understood by the reformers to have a double sense, the candidate being subject or object of the confirming. He is subject when he confesses his faith and goes on to confirm the baptismal vows. He is object when the Holy Spirit strengthens or confirms him in the faith. The Anglican Order of Confirmation in the Book of Common Prayer reveals this twofold sense. A very brief service calls upon the candidates to renew the vows made in their name at baptism. Then follows a prayer containing the petition for the Holy Spirit: "Strengthen them, we beseech thee, O Lord, with the Holy Ghost, the Comforter, and daily increase in them thy manifold gifts of grace . . . " with careful avoidance of the suggestion that anything is added now which was not already present in baptism. The imposition of hands too is accompanied by a carefully worded prayer that the candidate may "increase in thy Holy Spirit more and more."

Attempts at revision have revealed the differences which exist within the Anglican Church concerning the exact meaning of the rite of confirmation. "The Final Reports of the Joint Committees on Baptism, Confirmation and Holy Communion of the Convocations of Canterbury and York" submitted an order of initiation for an adult who had not yet been baptized. This order has the virtue of restoring the unity of the whole initiation, including baptism and confirmation. The part of the service for confirmation follows closely the Prayer Book order. But three members of the Canterbury Joint Committee submitted a minority report in which confirmation included consignation and the prayer for strengthening by the Holy Spirit was replaced by "Send down from heaven we beseech thee, O Lord, upon them thy Holy Ghost the Comforter. . . . " This report was submitted in 1954. In 1958 a report submitted by the Church of England Liturgical Commission suggested to the archbishops a form of service for the ministration of baptism and confirmation to those who are of age to answer for themselves. After baptism in this order follow consignation and then confirmation, with the prayer "Send down from heaven upon them thy Holy Ghost . . . " in a form which makes a clear distinction between water baptism and the coming of the Spirit. In the order suggested for confirmation it is stated that the candidate comes to *receive* the Spirit, and a clear difference is established between baptism with water for regeneration and confirmation by the outpouring of the Holy Spirit. The minority opinion of 1954 seems to have prevailed in the Liturgical Commission by 1958.

The Standing Liturgical Commission of the Protestant Episcopal Church in the United States of America, which published in 1950 its suggestions for discussion and consideration, follows a similar line in making confirmation the occasion when the Holy Spirit is *given* to the candidate. The distinction between baptism and the gift of the Spirit is emphasized by the reading of Acts 8:14-17. The tendency in both the Protestant Episcopal and Anglican churches is plainly toward making baptism an incomplete rite, since the gift of the Holy Spirit is conferred through confirmation.

The Presbyterian churches have always emphasized confirmation as simply a confirmation of baptism, in which the candidate makes vows and confesses his faith. There is no imposition of hands, and the only suggestion of confirmation in the objective sense is in the prayer asking for strength to be given by the Holy Spirit, with increase of grace.

D

John Wesley's works make little reference to confirmation. He refutes the Roman claim that it is a sacrament in his treatise "A Roman Catechism, faithfully drawn out of the allowed writings of the Church of Rome, with a Reply Thereto," but adds nothing constructive to the refutation. His other reference is in the long letter of November 26, 1762, to Dr. Warburton, Bishop of Gloucester. Speaking of the claim that the people of England are Christians, he wrote: "It must be allowed that the people of England generally have been christened or baptized; but neither can we infer,

'These were once baptized, therefore they are Christians now.'" He closed this point thus: "If men are not Christians until they are renewed after the image of Christ, and if the people of England in general are not thus renewed, why do we term them so?" He then proceeded to show that this renewal is the work of the Holy Spirit, by whom we are born again and assured of our adoption as sons. He went on to use the offices of the Church of England to illustrate his point, among them drawing three quotations, one from the office for baptism of infants, one from baptism "for those of Riper Years," and one from the Order of Confirmation:

> Give thy Holy Spirit to this infant, that he may be born again.
>
> Give thy Holy Spirit to these persons [already baptized] that they may continue as thy servants.
>
> Almighty God, who dost vouchsafe to regenerate these persons by water and the Holy Ghost, strengthen them with the Holy Ghost the Comforter, and daily increase in them the manifold gifts of thy grace.

"From these passages," he wrote, "it may sufficiently appear for what purposes every Christian . . . does now receive the Holy Ghost."

Wesley was not primarily discussing baptism and confirmation here, so that the references to the latter cannot be taken to be his opinion on the subject. As far as it goes, this letter appears to maintain the Holy Spirit is *given* in baptism for the purpose of regeneration, but the *continued* work of the Spirit leads a man to the new birth, assurance, and sanctification. In confirmation prayer is offered that the Spirit may produce this continued work.

While Methodism remained a society within the church the question of confirmation did not arise, but the separation of the Methodists into a church meant that the entry into the society of people who hitherto had not been members of the church became entry into an active membership of the church, and some service appropriate to mark this fact was necessary. The title of the forms of service which have been developed on both sides of the Atlantic plainly states its intention: "For The Public Recognition of New

Members" or "The Order for Receiving Persons into the Church" —and the stress has been placed on the confirmation of baptismal vows and on the fellowship of the church. The emphasis on welcome and fellowship has been in the past shown in the rite of the "right hand of fellowship," in place of imposition of hands. The present Book of Offices authorized by the British Conference includes in the order for The Public Reception of New Members:

1. A constitution of the Church; with thanksgiving and intercession for the Church;
2. Confession of faith;
3. Promises, including confirmation of the candidates' "response to His gracious call," engaging him "to be His faithful soldier and servant to your life's end"—an obvious reference to baptism;
4. Welcome, including blessing of confirmation—to "stablish, strengthen, settle" the candidate (but without express mention of the Holy Spirit);
5. Dedication of the whole congregation present;
6. Holy Communion.

The subjective and objective elements in confirmation are thus included; but there is no mention of any specific rite of imposition of hands or right hand of fellowship.

When considered with baptism as the whole rite of initiation into the church, this service appears to find its main deficiency in the catechumenate. This deficiency is lessened, however, when we consider what must be taken into account in confirmation, the conditions of membership in the Church. These are the desire to be saved from one's sins, the plain evidence of this in life and conduct, and the desire for fellowship with Christ and his Church. The second and third conditions argue for a trial period when these points can be tested, a period which should also be used for instruction. Thus provision is made for an adequate catechumenate. In *The Book of Worship for Church and Home,* published under the direction of the General Conference of The Methodist Church in America, the catechumenate is stressed by providing an order of service "For Receiving Persons as Preparatory Members."

Methodism therefore has in its usages, or at least within its grasp, all the elements of Christian initiation. The two main divisions are there—baptism, usually of infants; and confirmation, under the name of "Reception into Membership." The latter term is descriptive, but it has against it the fact that at baptism the child is received into the "congregation of Christ's flock" and so becomes a member of the Church. The statement on membership authorized by the British Conference in 1961 differentiates clearly between this and full membership, but this distinction affirms that membership begins at baptism and merely points to two types of membership. It seems better to think of the whole initiation, beginning with baptism and ending with the first communion, as reception into the membership of the Church, and to find another term for the rite which we now call "The Public Reception of New Members." The term "confirmation" lies at hand and has centuries of Protestant use to commend it.

It now remains for us to consider what we are trying to do in the whole process of receiving members into the Church and how far our orders of service achieve these aims.

E

Recent emphasis on the laity, with discussions of the function of members of the Church under the heading of the "Theology of the Laity," and references to confirmation as the "Ordination of the Laity," is in general a revival of interest in the doctrine of the priesthood of all believers. The way to the ordained ministry of the Church, if this doctrine is taken seriously, lies in first becoming a member of the whole Christian priesthood and then being ordained to the special ministry. Ordination does not make a man a priest; he becomes a priest when he joins the believing community of the Church. Ordination directs the way in which his priesthood is to be exercised. The priesthood of all believers is a corollary to Paul's conception of baptism as union with Christ in his death and resurrection, his constant references to the believer's being "in Christ," and to the view of the Church as the Body of Christ. The constitution of the Church and the place of the believer in the *koinonia* of the Church are to be determined in the light of the ministry and work of Christ.

The term which Jesus chose to describe his own ministry was *diakonia* (Matt. 20:25-28; Luke 22:27; cf. John 13). "Ministry," therefore, expresses the nature of the Body of Christ and the function of those who are united with him. Just as through Christ's *diakonia* the redemptive rule of God is established in the world, so through the *diakonia* of those who are Christ's the kingdom is being brought within the reach of every man. Membership in the Church therefore means partaking in this ministry. A member is incorporated into Christ and into his royal, prophetic, and priestly offices. Wesley was keenly aware of this and, driven by necessity as well as theology, placed great responsibility for the Christian mission on the shoulders of the lay members of the Church. This realization and practice has been the strength of Methodism.

This ministry in union with Christ has its creative source in the Holy Spirit. The reality of the indwelling Christ is made more and more apparent through the continuous revealing work of the Spirit. By the fortifying power of the Spirit the member of Christ is transformed "into the same image from glory to glory," as Paul put it (II Cor. 3:18 K.J.V.). So to be "in Christ" is also to be "in the Spirit." The Spirit in us also means Christ in us. Not that they are confused—the creative cause, the instructing intelligence, the persistent power, are the Spirit who is the energy and the endowments of the new life; the object and the content of the new life is Christ.

This participation in the Spirit is also a fellowship in the Spirit. Union with Christ through the Spirit means also union with one another through the same Spirit. The beginning of Methodism in societies made fellowship one of the main features of our church. Some have been sarcastic at our expense, suggesting that the only contribution that Methodism has to make to a world Church is the warm handshake. But if the handshake is truly symbolic of Christian fellowship, it may prove to be the greatest of all contributions. Christian fellowship is one experience of the Church which can be shared by *all* its members, even by those whose contribution to its ministry and mission is of necessity little or nothing.

In fact, that is the point at which we begin; when we can contribute nothing Christian love is extended to us. Infant baptism for most of us marks our entry into the Church. This should be the beginning of our catechumenate through the years when we grow in the fellowship of the Church and are instructed in its ways. At some point in the course of it there is the decisive moment when the continuance of the work and of the whole experience is our decision. And at last we reach the moment when we can take up the ministry of the Church, completing our unity with Christ begun when we were baptized into his death and resurrection, by receiving the bread and wine and, remembering his death and passion, becoming partakers of his body and blood. This whole experience, extending over many years, is our entry into the membership of the Church. We need to increase our sense of the unity of this experience.

When we receive "new members" we recall the baptism formula and ask for some renewal of the vows then made, so that some link is established between the beginning and the end of the period of becoming a member of the Church. Similarly in the baptism order the questions addressed to the parents and to the Church point forward to the period of training. These necessarily form a tenuous link, if only by reason of the passage of time between them. An excellent further link is provided in the "Order for Receiving Persons as Preparatory Members" in the American offices, and the similar order accepted by the British Conference in 1961. The Church in general, however, needs to see the process from infant baptism to the first communion as a whole, so that the responsibilities of the Church during this one process may be more clearly envisaged. This whole view could be encouraged by our preaching on the subject of initiation, for instance, at a baptismal service; it could be advanced to give a closer bond with the Church to Sunday school and youth work; it could be the subject of conferences of all church workers. It is also possible that future revisions of the Book of Offices may pay more regard to this unity.

More emphasis on the work of the Holy Spirit should find a place in our office. It is surprising that Wesley's emphasis on the continuing work of the Spirit in assurance and sanctification has no significant place in the service.

The other point which seems to lack significant emphasis in our present orders of service for receiving people into the full membership of the Church is that the candidate is entering a *diakonia*. He is essentially taking his place in a priesthood, with a ministry to accept and fulfill according to his ability. While this is lacking in our orders of service, it would be well to emphasize it in supplementary homilies, until a revision of the office can make more adequate provision than at present.

There is no suggestion here that baptism is in itself incomplete. It is the beginning of the way and brings the candidate into the Church, claiming all the work of Christ for him. We can never claim that an additional rite is necessary to salvation. What we can claim is that the Church knows its *full* members among those who after baptism have been instructed, have made their promises and under the guidance and strengthening of the Holy Spirit have accepted responsibility for the ministry of the Church, by their own confession and communion joining themselves to Christ in the fellowship of his people.

We can conclude with the analogy with which we began. The initiative lies with God, who chooses his people. They were "baptized into the fellowship of Moses in the cloud and sea." In the beginning of their way they knew little or nothing; the *fact* of redemption and the *promises* for the future were enough to start with. They had a long way to go and much to learn. Even then, only some of them came into a definite realization of what it meant to be the People of God. It is that realization for increasing numbers of those who have been baptized that is our subject when we think of confirmation and the "lay membership" of the Church.

7

Ordination and the Ministry in the Church

PHILIP S. WATSON

The Christian community, the Church, is described in scripture as the offspring of Abraham (Gal. 3:29), the spiritual kindred of Isaac (Gal. 4:28 ff.), and the Israel of God (Gal. 6:16). (Scripture quotations in this chapter are from the Revised Standard Version of the Bible.) Ancient Israel was the People of God under the old covenant established through Moses, and the Church is the same people under the new covenant established by Christ. It is true that most of the Jewish descendants of Israel have rejected Christ, but this only shows that "not all who are descended from Israel belong to Israel, and not all are children of Abraham because they are his descendants" (Rom. 9:6-7). Instead, the true Israel are those who share the faith of Abraham. The People of God is like an olive tree, long ago planted by God (Rom. 11:17 ff.). From it many of the natural branches (the Jews) have been broken off, and wild olive branches (Gentiles) have been grafted in. Thus the Gentiles who have accepted Christ have become members of the commonwealth of Israel, fellow citizens with the saints, and members of the household of God (Eph. 2:12, 19), while the Jews who have rejected Christ have forfeited these privileges—at least till they turn to Christ.

In the Church, the Israel of God, everything depends on Christ, and so close and entire is the dependence that the Church can be called the Body of Christ. Moreover, since Christ, its head, is the second Adam, it can also be called the New Man. It is a new humanity, a new creation of God, in which the old, deep wounds of mankind are healed, the divisions between Jew and Gentile, Greek and barbarian, and the rest are overcome. In contrast to this Body of Christ there stands another, the body of the flesh, of sin and of death (Col. 2:11; Rom. 6:6; 7:24), which is the body of fallen, sinful humanity, the first Adam, the Old Man, of which we are all members by our natural birth. Out of this old humanity the new is being fashioned by the incorporation of the children of Adam into the Body of Christ, so that they may become children of God by sharing in the life of his Son. The ordinary means of incorporation is baptism, and central to the life of the Body is the Lord's Supper, the communion of Christ's body and blood. Both of these are inseparably bound up with the preaching of the gospel, the Word of God, whereby men are called to repentance and faith and invited to participation in the sacraments. In this way the life of the Head is imparted to the Body and all its members. The members are, of course, very diverse, and they must be so, for they have different functions to perform within the unity of the Body (I Cor. 12:14 ff.). Sharing in the common life, each has his own ministry to fulfill, according to the gifts and graces he possesses, for the building up of the Body.

This Body of Christ is further described as the Temple of the Holy Spirit (I Cor. 3:16-17). It is a building "not made with hands," which is being raised as "a dwelling place of God in the Spirit," a "spiritual house" into which Christians are being built as "living stones," and within which they serve as a holy and royal priesthood (Eph. 2:19 ff.; I Pet. 2:4 ff.). In it Gentiles have equal rights with Jews, since both have access in one Spirit to the Father. The Spirit is imparted to the Church, today as at Pentecost, by Christ, its head, who is himself a "life-giving Spirit" (I Cor. 15:45), and the manifest signs and means of his spiritual presence and activity are the word and sacraments of the gospel. The word is the sword of the Spirit (Eph. 6:17); by one Spirit we were all baptized into the one Body (I Cor. 12:13); and the bread and wine of the Eucharist are spiritual food and drink (cf. I Cor. 10:3 ff.). Admittedly, not all who hear the word and partake of the sacraments actually receive the Spirit. They are in a sense "in the Spirit," as being in the sphere where the Spirit dwells, the Temple of Christ's Body. But the Spirit is not necessarily in them, and in that sense they are not "in the Spirit." The Spirit does not force himself on anyone; he is received only by faith; that is, by openness to his influence. To those who do receive him, however, he imparts a considerable variety of gifts and graces (I Cor. 12:4 ff.), which are intended, not for private use or enjoyment, but "for the work of ministry, for building up the body of Christ" (Eph. 4:12).

Now the Church, the Temple of Christ's Body and the Israel of God under the new covenant, is the heir to the promises God made to ancient Israel, and one of these promises in particular claims our attention here. When God established the old covenant at Sinai he promised his people that they should be a kingdom of priests and a holy nation (Exod. 19:6)—or as Isaiah put it generations later:

> . . . you shall be called the priests of the Lord,
> men shall speak of you as the ministers of our God." (Isa. 61:6.)

Under the old covenant, however, this promise was not to be fulfilled, but instead the Levitical priesthood was instituted as an example and reminder of what all Israel was meant to be.

Concerning this priesthood it is said in the book of Deuteronomy:

They shall teach Jacob thy ordinances,
and Israel thy law;
they shall put incense before thee,
and whole burnt offering upon thy altar. (Deut. 33:10.)

The task of the priesthood was thus twofold: The priests were to speak to men in the name of God, teaching them the divine will, and to approach God on behalf of men, presenting their offerings and sacrifices to him. Their role was mediatorial.

In earliest times, however, it seems that the primary function of the priest was to teach, to speak God's word to men. Naturally he also offered sacrifice, but this was not his exclusive prerogative—as probably teaching was not either. A man who was not a member of the official priesthood—especially if he were the head of a household—could very well perform the sacrificial rites, and he was certainly expected to teach at least his family what he knew of the will and way of God. In later times, however, for a variety of reasons, the offering of sacrifice became a virtual monopoly of the priesthood. What is more, as the priesthood became increasingly preoccupied with the sacrificial rites, the teaching aspect of the office came to be increasingly neglected. This is the chief burden of the prophetic complaint against the priests, that they no longer teach the people. At the same time, the sacrificial system itself became subject to abuse, against which the prophets had also vigorously to protest. In origin and in essence the offering of sacrifice is an occasion and a means of establishing, strengthening, or restoring communion between God and man. But it easily comes to be conceived as an instrument at the disposal of man, something he can manipulate in order to exert an influence on God and get his own way with him. It was just such a perversion of the idea of sacrifice that aroused the prophetic ire, but it was a perversion which need not have arisen had the priests done the job of teaching which the prophets, and after them the author of Deuteronomy, saw as their primary task.

The priesthood, however, was little amended by the prophetic rebukes. The priests continued to monopolize, and to be monopolized by, the sacrificial cultus. They let the teaching aspect of their office lapse into the hands of the scribes and Pharisees, who in their way were the successors of the prophets. In consequence, the fulfillment of God's promise that his people should be a kingdom of priests had to wait on the establishment of the new covenant through the priestly mediation and sacrifice of Christ.

Under the new covenant the old Levitical priesthood was done away, and the People of God became truly a royal priesthood and a holy nation (I Pet. 2:9). Then there was no special priesthood any longer because all Christians were priests. There was a special ministry of pastors and teachers charged with the responsibility of leading and guiding the whole priestly life of the Church, but there was no class of persons within the Church who were specially called priests. Instead, the whole Church as the Body of Christ, and every individual member of it, shared in the priestly dignity and calling of Christ, its head. So it was at any rate in the New Testament Church, and so it must always be if the Church is to be truly the Church.

This means that the Church, like the old Levitical priesthood, has a dual role to fulfill. It is called, on the one hand, to "offer spiritual sacrifices" to God, and on the other, to "declare the wonderful deeds" of God to men (I Pet. 2:5, 9). Its function, in other words, is mediatorial—as we might expect, seeing it is the Body of Christ, the one mediator between God and man. Moreover, every member of the Church shares in this priestly task, inasmuch as he shares in the priestly character of the Body. By his baptism, the act of his incorporation into the Body, he has been consecrated to this priesthood. Therefore, according to his ability and opportunity, it is his business to bear witness both by word and deed to the truth of God in Christ and to intercede with both prayer and self-sacrificing service for the world. This is the calling of the whole Church, in which every member has his part to play. The part of the "ministers and clergy," as we call them, is to lead and guide the laity in the fulfillment of its priestly service.

The Church's priestly vocation is epitomized in the central act of Christian worship, the Lord's Supper. Here we proclaim the Lord's death till he come (I Cor. 11:26), setting forth the gospel in dramatic rite and declaring the most wonderful of all the wonderful deeds of God. Here also we offer spiritual sacrifices to God—our prayers and praises, our alms and oblations, our souls and bodies—to be used in his service, as our grateful response to the grace he has shown to us. The priestly service of the Church, however, while it centers in the Lord's Supper, does not end there. It goes out into all the world, where Christians in every walk of life have the duty and privilege of witnessing, not only with their lips, but with their lives, to the truth of God in Christ, and just in this way offering their spiritual sacrifices to God. Not everyone is able, however, nor should everyone desire, to play the same part; for while all share alike in the one, common priesthood of the Body of Christ, yet precisely as members of the Body they are and must be diverse in function and service. There is only one priesthood, but there are many ministries or forms of service.

The different forms of ministry, however, are not all of equal importance, and there is one form in particular on which it must be said that all the rest depend; namely, the ministry of the Word. This means, in the first instance of course, the ministry of Christ himself, the Incarnate Word, without which there would never have been any Church or Christian priestly community with its manifold arms of ministry. Christ is the first and supreme minister in the Church. He is the Son of man, who "came not to be served, but to serve, and to give his life as a ransom for many" (Mark 10:45). He is the Son of God, "who . . . did not count equality with God a thing to be grasped, but emptied himself, taking the form of a servant . . . and became obedient unto death, even death on a cross" (Phil. 2:6-8). He is the good shepherd, the *bonus pastor*, who gives his life for the sheep (John 10:14-15). To this end he has come from God, has been sent by God, and it is his meat to do the will of him that sent him.

Christ is thus the source and pattern of all ministry in the Church, as he ministers to mankind at the cost of his life. We should notice, however, that he serves men not by submitting himself to them as if they were his masters, but by being the Suffering Servant of the Lord. His service of men consists, not in doing their will, but his heavenly Father's. Consequently, in all his ministering and serving he speaks and acts with authority. He is "a prophet mighty in deed and word" (Luke 24:19), at whose authority men exclaim with astonishment, and when they ask him where he gets it, he makes it plain that they must understand his authority to come from God (Mark 11:27-33).

But our Lord does not exercise this ministerial authority alone, by himself. Even in the days of his flesh he conferred similar authority on others, the disciples he chose out of the crowds that followed him, and sent them forth to share in the same ministry. These were his messengers, his representatives, as he was God's, and therefore he could tell them, "He who receives you receives me, and he who receives me receives him who sent me" (Matt. 10:40). The commission he gave them, however, was limited to the territory of Israel, and when they had fulfilled it they returned to him. Then after his resurrection the authorization and sending out of his representatives is resumed, and on a vastly wider scale. Now he is able to declare, "All authority in heaven and on earth has been given to me. Go therefore and make disciples of all nations . . . ." (Matt. 28:18-19). Consequently, when the apostles are asked by what authority they act, they can reply that it is by his authority (Acts 9:15). They are servants (*douloi*) of Jesus Christ and ministers (*diakonoi*) of the new covenant (Phil. 1:1; II Cor. 3:6). They speak and act on behalf of Christ and are, as it were, the mouthpieces of God (II Cor. 5:20-21). They have been chosen and sent for service (*diakonia*—ministry), but for the service of the Word, not the serving of tables (Acts 6:1-7).

Yet neither do the apostles, any more than our Lord, exercise their ministerial authority alone. Where they come and are received others are raised up to assist them in their work and to carry it on after them—prophets, evangelists, teachers, administrators, pastors. And when other forms of ministry change and pass away, the pastoral office remains, to which men are ordained and charged with the ministry of the Word and sacraments (as we commonly call it). That is not, of course, a New Testament phrase, and it is in some ways an unfortunate one. For the moment, however, we may let it stand while we take note of several important developments in connection with this ministry during the early centuries of the Church.

First, the pastoral office quickly developed a threefold structure—bishop, presbyter, and deacon—of which the beginnings are discernible already in the New Testament. It is true that in the New Testament the distinction between bishop and presbyter is by no means sharp; in fact, the terms are virtually interchangeable. This is hardly surprising in view of the fact that one and the same person can very well have both the status of a presbyter, or elder, and the function of an *episcopos,* a superintendent or bishop. Before long, however, a distinction came to be drawn between bishops as superintending elders and presbyters as elders under their superintendency; an arrangement which was natural enough, no doubt, as the Church increased in numbers and had to meet the needs of changing circumstances. Nor was it unreasonable that bishops were regarded as successors of the apostles, and in some sense inheritors of their apostolic authority, while the presbyters were assistants and representatives of the bishops. After all, the apostles themselves had appointed superintending elders—or presbyter-bishops—in the churches they had personally founded, and it was natural that these should have the responsibility of appointing others as need arose to work with them or to carry on the work after them. Quite understandably, therefore, the right to administer ordination came to be ordinarily reserved to the superintending elder, the bishop.

A second important development was the practice that arose very early in the Church of describing the ordained ministers as priests and distinguishing them as such from the laity. This was chiefly due, no doubt, to the fact that the Old Testament, with its account of the Levitical priesthood, was for long the only scripture the Church possessed, and since neither Jewish nor Gentile Christians were at all accustomed to the idea of a religion without a special priesthood, they were predisposed to follow the Old Testament pattern. In consequence, from the time of Clement of Rome onward the thought of the priesthood of all Christians—the "universal priesthood"—fell more and more into the background, while the clergy gradually gained what amounted to a monopoly of priestly functions.

A third development, which had even more serious consequences, was a change that took place in the understanding of the priestly functions themselves. Owing once more, no doubt, to both Jewish and Gentile preconceptions, for which the primary business of priesthood was the offering of sacrifice, the Eucharist, over which the bishop or superintending elder naturally presided, came to be interpreted as an atoning or propitiatory sacrifice offered to God on behalf of the living and the dead. That is to say, the priestly self-offering of the Church in gratitude to God and for his service in the world gave place to an offering by the ordained priest of the consecrated bread and wine, the body and blood of Christ, on behalf of the Church. Moreover, the offering of this sacrifice came to be the primary function of the ordained priest. This change, which had already taken place by the time of Cyprian in the third century, marks a distinct departure from the second-century position of Irenaeus and Tertullian, for whom the clergy—and especially the bishops, as successors of the apostles—were chiefly the guardians and guarantors of the purity of the apostolic teaching.

A fourth development, first clearly seen in Augustine, was the understanding of ordination to the priesthood as a sacramental act whereby the person ordained receives a *character indelebilis,* an indelible mark, which sets him permanently apart from the laity. Once a priest he is always a priest and can never revert to the status of a layman. This idea stems no doubt in part from the conviction, which has almost certainly existed from the beginning, that the work of the ministry demands total commitment, and that ordination to it implies acceptance of a life-long vocation. More than this is implied, however, when the ministry is understood as an exclusive priesthood, for by virtue of the *sacramentum ordinis,* or sacrament of order, administered by a bishop, the priest is empowered to administer the other sacraments as a layman is not—except that in emergency situations a layman may administer baptism. With that exception, the validity of the other sacraments is made to depend on the priestly *character* of the celebrant.

The fifth and final development we must notice is found in the late fifth-century writings on the heavenly and ecclesiastical hierarchies that go under the name of Dionysius the Areopagite. What we have to observe here is a very considerable enhancement of the position of the bishop, who already had special importance in the Church as alone having the right to ordain. According to Dionysius the bishop holds the highest rank in the ecclesiastical hierarchy and is inferior only to the angels, who are the lowest in the heavenly hierarchy. Therefore, the bishop forms the indispensable link between earth and heaven. Through the bishop the divine powers of salvation that stream down through the various orders of the heavenly hierarchy are mediated sacramentally to the lower orders of the ecclesiastical—the priests, deacons, monks, baptized Christians, and catechumens in turn. Consequently, where there is no properly consecrated bishop or where the bishop fails to fulfill his sacramental functions, there can be no mediation of sacramental, saving grace—an idea which has not infrequently been echoed in modern ecumenical discussions.

Now such a doctrine of the ministry as this, for which there is no vestige of support in the New Testament, we cannot but reject, as the Reformers did. By their time a situation had arisen in the New Israel comparable with that which existed in the Old Israel in the time of the prophets and of our Lord. The priests were preoccupied with the cultus, which centered in the sacrifice of the mass; their teaching office was practically forgotten, or at best was fulfilled in terms of a scholastic theology only too reminiscent of the spirit of the scribes and Pharisees. The thought of the priestly vocation of the whole Church and of every Christian scarcely entered into anyone's head. Against all this the Reformers raised their protest like the prophets of old, seeking to recall the clergy to their true ministry as servants of the Word of God, and to restore the true nature of the Church as a priestly community ordered and governed by that Word. For the most part the churches that have followed them have ceased to call their ministers or clergy "priests," though they have never very fully grasped the meaning of the universal priesthood of the Church, and in consequence, it has often seemed among them that neither clergy nor laity were priests.

As we have already seen, the function of priesthood is mediatorial and involves a movement in two directions, from God to man and from man to God. We have also seen that under both the old covenant and the new those who were specially called priests came to be almost exclusively concerned with the second movement, so that prophets and reformers had to be raised up to redress the balance. The resulting conflicts, however, between the priests and the prophets and reformers unhappily gave rise to the idea that the prophetic and the priestly ministries are, if not mutually exclusive, at least quite distinct and separate. This idea was maintained by John Wesley, for example, in his sermon on "The Ministerial Office," when he told his lay preachers that they were of the order of prophets, not priests, and that, therefore, they had no right to administer the sacraments. That right belonged only to the regularly ordained clergy, the priests of the Church of England. It was true that the clergy ought also to have been fulfilling the prophetic ministry which had devolved upon the Methodist preachers, and the latter must herefore be regarded as "*extraordinary messengers,* raised up to provoke the *ordinary* ones to jealousy." Yet even when exercised by one and the same person the two ministries, prophetic and priestly, remained in Wesley's view totally distinct. It seems odd that Wesley could not conceive of the "extraordinary" call of his preachers as including also the administration of the sacraments, seeing that this was hardly more effectively done in eighteenth-century Anglicanism than the preaching of the Word. There appears to be something of an unreformed hangover in the Anglican Wesley here.

Be that as it may, this kind of distinction between the prophetic and the priestly office is, to say the least, very misleading. It not only improperly limits the meaning of priesthood, but it also encourages a separation between the Word and the sacraments of the gospel which is thoroughly false. We have already suggested that the phrase "the Word and sacraments" is an unfortunate one, and it is so not least because it too easily leads to the equation of the Word of God simply with words. The Word of God is, of course, expressed in words—the written words of scripture and the spoken words of Christian preaching and teaching—but it is also expressed in the dramatic actions of baptism and the Lord's Supper—those sacraments of the gospel which, in Augustine's vivid phrase, can be called "visible words." Or to put it another way, both the Word and the sacraments, as we ordinarily speak of them, are signs and means of the presence and activity of Jesus Christ, the Incarnate Word of God, who alone is the Word in the full and proper sense of the term. Therefore they belong inseparably together. What is more, they both belong to the prophetic rather than the priestly office—if those two are distinguished in the way we have just described as wrong—for both represent the manward movement of God rather than the Godward movement of man. They do not exclude the Godward movement of course, but they rather furnish the ground and motivation of it.

Now the ordained ministry exists in order precisely that the Word of God may be brought to men by the Word and sacraments of the gospel and that men may be brought to God through Christ and made living members of the holy and royal priesthood which is Christ's Body, the Church. For that reason, the office of the ministry has from the beginning been characterized by the same notes of authority and service that we have seen in the ministry of our Lord and his apostles (cf. I Cor. 16:15-16; I Thess. 5:12; Heb. 13:7, 17; I Pet. 5:2-3). It is true that all Christians have the duty and privilege of bearing witness to Christ in all the ways they can, and it is also true that the Church can authorize, in case of need, unordained laymen to preach or administer the sacraments. Indeed, as Luther says in his "Address to the German Nobility," if a group of Christians were cut off from the rest of the Church without an ordained minister among them they would have the right to authorize one of their own number to be their minister in holy things, and they would have this right because they are all already priests and, therefore, in principle qualified to deal with holy things. Ordinarily, however, this authority belongs to the ministerial office and is conferred by ordination at the hands of those already ordained to the office.

Ordination is the commission of Christ, the head of the Body, conferred on certain members of his Body, to ensure the perpetuation of his own ministry, the ministry of the Word. Although this ministry is the general responsibility of the whole Church, it is necessary that there should be such special commissioning, partly in order to avoid the risk of everybody's business becoming nobody's business, and partly to prevent the confusion and disorder that could result from lack of duly authorized leadership. Ordination does not confer any special priestly powers on the minister, who is neither more nor less a priest than any other Christian, but inasmuch as it implies total commitment and a life-long vocation, the thought of it as unrepeatable and even as imparting a *character indelebilis* may not be too wide of the mark. It does, moreover, confer upon the minister an authority which, although it is conferred through his fellow members in the Church, is not derived from them, but is given him by Christ. The minister is not the elected representative or delegate of an ecclesiastical democracy, and thus a servant of the people's will. He is a servant of Jesus Christ, and he serves his people best when both he and they remember that if he is also their servant it is "for Jesus' sake" (II Cor. 4:5).

In none of this does ordination give the minister any monopoly or exclusive rights. It is probably quite wrong to ask, as people so often do, what there is that an ordained minister can do which a layman cannot or ought not do. The purpose of having an ordained ministry is not to establish any monopoly of ministering, but to ensure that the ministry shall be carried on. The minister, therefore, has the responsibility of seeing that it is carried on. He is, we might well say, a leading layman; he is a member of the *laos* or People of God, appointed to lead and guide that people in the priestly service of God and man to which they are one and all called. Hence the minister's authority is not given him in order that he may lord it over his people, but in order that he may more effectively serve. His authority does not belong to him personally, but to his office, and he has no claim to it except as he duly and faithfully fulfills the functions of that office. Here we must bear in mind the scriptural warnings against "false apostles" and "false teachers," who pervert the gospel and have therefore no authority to which the people ought to submit (II Cor. 11:1-6, 12-15), and we may recall that even a true apostle like Peter is not infallible and may, therefore, sometimes have to be resisted, as Paul resisted him at Antioch (Gal. 2:11 ff.). In a similar way the leaders of the Reformation and the Evangelical Revival had in their day to resist the clergy—and especially the bishops, the lordly successors of the apostles, who no longer understood the nature of the apostolic ministry to which they were called.

As a result of this resistance, of course, most of the churches that sprang from the Reformation and the Revival lost, whether by accident or design, the traditional threefold structure of the ministry. This fact presents us with one of the chief and most intractable problems today with regard to the unity of the Church. In this connection two things must be said. First, those who regard the threefold—or indeed any other—structure as essential so that there cannot be any true ministry without it would do well to consider our Lord's rebuke to his disciples when they forbade a man to cast out demons "because he does not follow with us" (Luke 9:49-50). This incident, we may recall, furnished the text for John Wesley's sermon "A Caution Against Bigotry," in which among other things he refused to unchurch those Christian communions which did not possess the same structure of ministry as his own—and incidentally, pleaded for a recognition of the ministry being carried out by his own irregular troops of preachers. As he insisted in his "Letter to a Clergyman" (May, 1748), "a doctor is one who heals" and "one who does not heal is not a doctor"; therefore, if a man without professional medical status fulfills the true function of a doctor his right to do so can hardly be questioned by professionals who are failing in their duty. So neither could the professional clergy complain if the Methodist preachers, unordained as they were, and out of the historical succession as they still are, fulfill the true function of the clergy.

This argument, however, cuts both ways, and therefore the second thing to be said is that those who no longer possess the traditional structure of the ministry might well ask themselves whether their own alternative to it really serves the function of the ministry any more effectively. This is a particularly important question at a time like the present, when the divisions of the Church obscure and distort the gospel which a divided world so sorely needs. In view of the fundamental importance of the ministry for the Church, the unity of the Church is unlikely to be achieved without the unification of the ministry, and seeing that the threefold structure —in the historic succession—is the oldest and most widespread in the Church, it has at least a strong claim to be considered as a basis for unification. Admittedly, we must maintain, as John Wesley did, that the uninterrupted succession of bishops is a fable, that an ordained presbyter is as much a scriptural *episcopos* as any bishop, and that, though the bishop may be ordinarily responsible for ordinations, he has no absolute and exclusive right in the matter. Ordination is a matter of order, not orders. But seeing there is disorder in the Church owing to our divided ministries must we not seek somehow to bring them into "full connexion" with one another, so that without denying the reality of any of them we may move toward a reform of all, with a view to their more effective functioning? If to this end we are asked to include a mutual laying on of hands with prayer for one another, need we be fearful of that? Provided it was clearly neither an act of ordination nor a prerequisite for our meeting together at the Lord's table, would it not be a fitting way of sealing the union of our different but equally valid ministries? After all, the laying on of hands is used in the New

Testament Church for other purposes than ordination, and even the Apostle Paul had hands laid on him more than once.

More important than all this, however, is to be clear about the nature of the minister's task, the service he is commissioned by his ordination to perform. Here we may well begin by recalling Paul's description of himself and his fellow workers as "ambassadors for Christ" (II Cor. 5:20). An ambassador, as we commonly use the term, is one sent to represent the government of his own country to a foreign power. It is his business to interpret the mind of his own government in terms the foreigners can understand. He has no right to any independent initiative or mind of his own in the matter; he has nothing to do but represent the mind of another as intelligently, efficiently, courteously, and loyally as he can. Just so every minister of the gospel is sent. He is sent on a mission of reconciliation, bearing a message of reconciliation from God to man, and as he carries out his duties as Christ's ambassador to a world estranged it is God himself who makes his appeal through him, beseeching men to be reconciled to God. When God's message of reconciliation is brought to men it is God's Word that men hear, even though the voice and the words are those of a man—and even if the hearers do not recognize it as God's Word.

The minister, then, is a preacher of God's Word, and in this connection there is another word of Paul that is peculiarly relevant. "What we preach," he said, "is not ourselves, but Jesus Christ as Lord, with ourselves as your servants for Jesus' sake (II Cor. 4:5). Everyone of course knows that it is not the business of the Christian preacher to preach "himself"; yet how often it seems to pass unnoticed by both the pulpit and the pew when preachers do just that—when they preach their own ideas, experiences, philosophies, or even their doubts! Such preachers may be interesting and even inspiring, but they are not preaching the Word of God. To preach the Word means to preach Jesus Christ as Lord. That is the unvarying theme of all Christian preaching, even though it is not always expressed in just those words. In the New Testament men preach many things—the gospel, the kingdom of God, the forgiveness of sins, the word of the cross, and so forth—but all these concepts are inseparably bound up with Jesus Christ and his Lordship. It is the business of the Christian preacher to "offer Christ" (Wesley) or to "portray Christ" (Luther), not to portray or offer himself in any shape or form; for it is Christ who is the Word of God. The texts of his sermons will of course vary, as do the situations to which he has to relate the message of Christ, but Christ will be his constant theme.

The preaching of the Word of God is not, of course, to be equated simply with the delivery of sermons. The Word is proclaimed also, as we have already said, when the sacraments are administered, which belong together with preaching. Furthermore, just as the ministry of the Word is not limited to sermons, so neither is it limited to occasions of public worship. It involves more particular pastoral care in which what is done publicly in church is applied more privately and intimately to individuals or groups. This brings us, finally, to the work of the minister as a pastor or shepherd of Christ's flock.

In the Old Testament Israel as the People of God is often likened to a flock of sheep. It is God's flock,

> . . . the people of his pasture,
> and the sheep of his hand. (Ps. 95:7.)

God, who has led this people like a shepherd out of Egypt (Ps. 77:20), is himself called the "Shepherd of Israel" (Ps. 80:1). But the human leaders of Israel, the rulers in Church and state, are also likened to shepherds, though they are not owners of the flock as God is. They are undershepherds in the service of the Owner. It is a wayward and unruly flock, and its shepherds are themselves often wayward too. They fail to recognize their responsibility; they exploit their position; they serve their own interests at the expense of the flock; they fleece and butcher the sheep; they destroy or scatter the flock. Therefore God promises that he will himself take action; he will punish the bad shepherds, restore the flock, and appoint other, good and faithful, shepherds for them (Ezek. 36:1-24). He will indeed himself shepherd his flock (Isa. 40:10-11; Ezek. 34:11-12).

This promise of God is fulfilled in Jesus Christ, who can say, "I am the good shepherd," the *bonus pastor* (John 10:11). Jesus more than once speaks of the relation between God and man as that between a shepherd and his sheep, and he says that he is himself sent "to the lost sheep of the house of Israel" (Matt. 15:24). He has compassion on the multitudes because they are "like sheep without a shepherd" (Mark 6:34). He calls his disciples his "little flock" (Luke 12:32) and is himself called "the great shepherd of the sheep" (Heb. 13:20) and "the chief Shepherd" (I Pet. 5:4). But there are also in the New Testament undershepherds. Peter is commissioned, "Feed my lambs. . . . Tend my sheep" (John 21:15 ff.). He in turn bade his fellow presbyters, "Tend the flock of God that is in your charge" (I Pet. 5:2), just as Paul exhorted the Ephesian elders, "Take heed to yourselves and to all the flock, in which the Holy Spirit has made you guardians [*episcopous*—bishops]" (Acts 20:28); and among the gifts of Christ to the Church there are numbered "pastors" (Eph. 4:11).

From passages like these we can sketch the character and aims of the pastoral ministry, the work of the minister as a shepherd of Christ's flock, and the spirit in which that work must be done. The shepherd here spoken of is one who leads, not drives, his flock, which it is his task both to feed and to guard. He knows his sheep and calls them by name. He strengthens the weak, cares for the injured, and carries the lambs in his arms. He watches over those who are well and strong to see that they keep well and strong, and to prevent their growing headstrong! He seeks out the lost, even the one lost sheep, having a care for each individual member of the flock, and teaching each of them to say, "The Lord is *my* shepherd." He has also other sheep besides those already within the fold, and these too must be gathered in. He has authority over the sheep, as being in charge of them. It is not his business to leave them to their own devices or to let them go as they please. At the same time, his authority is exercised in service. He carries out his duties in the spirit of Peter's words, "not by constraint but willingly, not for shameful gain but eagerly, not as domineering over those in your charge, but being examples to the flock" (I Pet. 5:23). He has heard the words of the chief Shepherd himself: "As the Father has sent me, even so I send you" (John 20:21)—to be good shepherds, good pastors. He remembers that the good shepherd lays down his life for the sheep.

8

The Lord's Supper

A. RAYMOND GEORGE

The revival of interest in the Lord's Supper is one of the most striking features of the current ecumenical scene, and in considering what doctrinal contribution Methodism can make to the whole ecumenical movement we ought to take a lively interest in this field. Moreover, our history entitles us to do this, for the sacramental practice and teaching of the Wesleys were an important part of their contribution to the century in which they lived and have still much to teach us. It would be a great mistake to draw some sharp opposition between sacramental and evangelical emphases and then simply to label the Wesleys as evangelical. Evangelical of course they were, but they were sacramentalists as well; indeed they are a preeminent example of the compatibility of these two trends. It has been the great service of J. E. Rattenbury to draw attention to the once neglected facts which abundantly attest this claim. Whether the Methodists of subsequent generations have successfully maintained this combination is another question, but the current ecumenical trend gives us a good opportunity to recover it.

We shall consider first the practice of the Wesleys and then two aspects of their doctrine, and under each heading shall relate the matter to the current ecumenical situation. It might be objected that we ought to start from the New Testament, but that would only duplicate work which has already been done. The Wesleys will serve at any rate as our starting point, but of course the New Testament will be present in our minds as the standard and norm.

The practice of John Wesley has been thoroughly investigated by John C. Bowmer in his book *The Sacrament of the Lord's Supper in Early Methodism*. In a later work *The Lord's Supper in Methodism, 1791-1960* he investigated the period after Wesley in British Methodism. Wesley's practice is summed up in the title of a sermon which he wrote before the Aldersgate experience in 1733 and published long after that experience, in 1788, the sermon on "The Duty of Constant Communion." The word "constant" he deliberately chose in preference to "frequent," which he regarded as inadequate. In this as in other matters he practiced what he preached. Thus in the year from June 1, 1740, to May 31, 1741, he received the communion at least forty times on Sundays and fifty-eight times on weekdays. In the last ten years of his life, despite considerable gaps, he received the communion on an average every five days. His practice varied a little according to where he was, but when he was in London he received the communion nearly every Sunday morning.

There was a certain development in the place of these communion services. At first they were in parish churches, in the English sense of that term; i.e., in the churches belonging to the Church of England. He would celebrate the communion elsewhere in only one case (apart from Anglican college chapels and the like); i.e., for a sick person in a private house. As his followers became less welcome in the parish churches, however, he began to celebrate more freely in private houses, then in Hugunot chapels, and finally in Methodist preaching houses or chapels. As early as 1741 in a French chapel in Wapping (an example of the intermediate stage), he arranged for his members, a thousand in number, to receive the communion two hundred a week in rotation.

In the provinces—apart from Bristol and Norwich—the development was much slower than in London. Toward the end of his life Wesley celebrated the communion in Methodist chapels in the provinces on his visits, but in his absence there was not usually an Anglican clergyman willing to do this, and the number of men ordained by Wesley for England was negligible. So Wesley was constantly urging the people to receive the communion at the parish churches, as indeed he sometimes did himself, even to the end of his life. The people were increasingly unwilling to follow his lead, however, nor was this surprising in view of the attitude of many of the Anglican clergy.

Thus we may broadly say that the norm, as demonstrated in London and in Wesley's own practice, was at least weekly communion.

This has not been maintained in British Methodism. A prime reason was the lack of ordained clergymen and then after Wesley's death the disputes which preceded the Plan of Pacification in 1795. This permitted the traveling preachers to administer the sacraments and thus virtually claimed for them the status of ordained ministers. Even then there were far more chapels than there were ministers, as in England there still are, and because of all these difficulties the people lost the habit of receiving the communion frequently. Indeed, in the provinces they may never have had the opportunity of acquiring it. Old circuit plans suggest that for a considerable period only the town chapels had communion services. Country Methodists separated themselves only gradually from the Church of England and, no doubt, went sometimes for communion to the parish church, as to this day some of them do for marriages and burials. At a later period fear of the so-called ritualism of the Oxford Movement and then of the growing influence of Romanism led to a further decline in sacramental practice. In America, similarly, the conditions in which the circuit riders worked so nobly on the frontier must have militated to some extent against settled sacramental observances.

Now the ecumenical scene presents something of a return to early Methodist practice. Roman churches, not content with passive attendance at Mass, are urging the people actually to receive the communion each Sunday. Anglican Churches are breaking away from the pattern that has prevailed in many of them for a century or so—the pattern of Holy Communion for the few at 8 A.M. and Morning Prayer for the many at 11 A.M.—and are increasingly having one main morning service including both preaching and communion, usually at 9:30 A.M. Continental Protestants are also ceasing to regard the communion as a sort of occasional appendage to the preaching service and are holding, often once a month, a full service of Word and sacrament. Karl Barth has described a service of preaching without the sacrament as a "torso," [1] and there would be widespread agreement among liturgical scholars that the normal full Christian service, which ideally would be the main service each Sunday morning, is a service which includes both the preaching of the Word and the celebration of the Lord's Supper.

Ought Methodism to approve of such a development? We have seen that it is in accordance with John Wesley's practice and, we might add, with the intentions of the Anglican Prayer Book and of Luther and Calvin, though Calvin was prevented by the magistrates at Geneva from carrying out his intention. But the real test must be the New Testament, and though it is nowhere formally stated in the New Testament that regular Sunday worship is to take this form, we can see from the New Testament itself (as has been shown by such books as O. Cullmann, *Early Christian Worship* and C. F. D. Moule, *Worship in the New Testament*) and from such writers as Justin that this was almost certainly the practice of the New Testament and quite certainly that of the early Church. A practice favored by the New Testament, the principal Reformers, and the Wesleys has strong claims on us. In each of these three cases it was

[1] *The Knowledge of God and the Service of God* (London: Hodder & Stoughton, Ltd., 1938), p. 211.

afterward modified, but we may perhaps ascribe that to human weakness rather than to any defect in the practice itself. We should therefore welcome the current ecumenical trend and encourage it within Methodism.

The first step should be to see that when communion is observed the service should be regarded as a single whole, Word and sacrament forming a kind of double climax. This does not mean that there can be no opportunity for the departure of those who do not wish to stay; there is ancient precedent for the dismissal of catechumens and excommunicate persons, though not for the departure of full members. People ought not, however, to be dragooned into being present at the communion. On the other hand, where the service does proceed without a break to the communion, as in some places is the practice, the congregation is often larger on such occasions than on other Sundays, which seems to give some support to the idea of completely omitting any pause.

The norm for such services should be that form of communion service which includes the elements of reading the scriptures and preaching. The first order in the British Book of Offices does this, and so does the first in the American Ritual, the one which springs, I believe, from the old Methodist Episcopal Church. In my judgment, however, the more conservative form of the prayer of consecration in the second American order, that from the old Methodist Episcopal Church, South, is to be preferred at that point. (The alteration of this prayer does not go far back, however, in the history of the old Methodist Episcopal Church.) Yet it is not essential to use these orders, so long as their main spirit is preserved. Indeed, the time is ripe for revision, such as that with which the American General Conference concerned itself in 1960. The British Conference also is likely to take the matter in hand; indeed, certain unofficial proposals are already circulating.

It would be too much to hope that in the near future such services could be held weekly in our churches, though as a theologian I think that is plainly the right course. It would not be too much to arrange them monthly, however, and so to order the service on other Sundays as to bring out the resemblance both in purpose and in structure between the communion service and the preaching service. This last point was suggested by the report of the Commission on Worship made to the British Conference in 1960.

Before we leave these matters of practice we might digress a little to consider certain other features of that aspect of the ecumenical movement which is called the liturgical movement. As well as the stress on the centrality of the communion service, in the sense of a full service of Word and sacrament, certain other notes are now commonly struck. Most of these concern the corporate nature of Christian worship. It is pointed out that *leitourgia* is derived, though somewhat indirectly, from *laos,* people, and *ergon,* work, and, though James Barr, in *The Semantics of Biblical Language,* has thrown some doubt on the value of such etymological arguments, the fact cannot be denied that worship is the task of the whole people of God. It is not something done by a body of clerics for the rank and file of the people; it is offered by the whole people of God, which includes ministers and what we call "laymen" alike, who all belong to a priestly body.

In Methodism we are apt to think that, as we undoubtedly believe in the priesthood of all believers, we are in no danger of an erroneous sacerdotalism and that therefore the liturgical movement has much to teach others but nothing to teach us. Our practice hardly bears this out, however. We do, indeed, at least in England, make extensive use of laymen as preachers, but when they are conducting worship they naturally act much as ministers do, and tend to dominate the worship. What is meant in ecumenical circles by the active participation of the laity is that the people of the congregation should take a more active part. Of course the singing of perhaps five of our great hymns gives them a part which is more significant than other communions perhaps realize, but we ought to be ready to consider some of the methods now used in other communions—the reading of the scripture by lay people, the opportunity given to the congregation to suggest subjects for intercession, the bringing up of the elements by representatives of the people, the corporate saying of the prayer of humble access, and so on. The people in our services need to be far less passive, and here *we* need to experiment just as much as do other traditions; we are more in danger than we realize of a false clericalism. By this I do not mean that the ordained ministry has no distinctive role; the priesthood of all believers does not mean that any believer may appropriately fulfill every type of ministry within the Church. But the ordained minister must not be so strongly set over against the people; although as preacher he must to some extent confront them, yet as leader of the more responsive part of worship he must rather be ringed round by others performing supporting ministries.

The phrase "ringed round" serves to introduce the current trend in ecclesiastical architecture. Instead of a Gothic-type chancel with its suggestion of God "out there" beyond the east window, we see now a reversion to the style of the early basilicas, where a free-standing table is surrounded by the chief minister and his assistants gathered on the one side and the rest of the people on the other sides. Methodism should welcome this.

This whole new stress on the corporate is congenial to our emphasis on fellowship. But it is opposed to that individualistic pietism which has sometimes intruded itself into Methodism, whereby the service is regarded simply as a means of doing good to the so-called souls of the individuals present, so that the only test of the validity of an act of worship comes to be whether the people present think they get any spiritual benefit from it, which can easily degenerate into whether the people like it or enjoy it. On this view, a variety of services is provided; like one selecting from a menu, you choose what suits you best. This attitude is now rightly replaced by the notion that it is the duty of God's people in any one place to gather together each Sunday to hear his Word and to offer him the worship which is his due, whatever their individual feelings may be. Incidentally, now that many British Methodists go to church only once on Sunday, choosing the morning or evening as suits them best, the question arises whether we should not eliminate this lack of corporateness by having only one main service. The American multiplicity of morning services might also be called in question were it not happily necessitated by the large size of the congregations.

Another note sounded by the liturgical movement is that of contemporaneity. We must speak to our own age and divest ourselves of the trappings of the Gothic, the eighteenth-century, or the Victorian era. The popularity of the New English Bible is a sign of this trend. It raises a delicate question, Which elements of worship are rooted in the gospel itself (the use of bread and wine, for instance, is surely a proper part of the scandal of particularity) and which may properly vary in varying ages and varying cultures (which in our overseas missionary work is known as the problem of the indigenization of worship)? In this respect we have probably been too conservative, though we must remember that worship gains dignity by a use of traditional elements; e.g., the robes of the ministers, even though these represent a tradition which does not go back to the gospel itself. We need not abandon the use of traditional music any more than we abandon Bach or Beethoven in the secular concert hall. Nor need we pull down historic buildings. But as a good concert will often contain not only Bach but also contemporary music, as side by side with ancient buildings modern buildings are erected and, indeed, to ancient buildings modern additions are made; so in music, in architecture, in translations of the Bible, and in the style of its prayers, the Church must ever seek to blend the new with the old. It was once asked, "Why should the devil have all the best tunes?" Thus we must claim for Christ's worship the best elements of contemporary culture and avoid giving the impression that to become a Christian is somehow to become a man of an earlier century.

From this digression we turn back to the Lord's Supper, and having considered matters of practice, we now come, in the second place, to matters of doctrine, and of these the first is its relation to sacrifice. It is often simply assumed that Romans and Anglo-Catholics regard the Eucharist as a sacrifice and Protestants regard it simply as a memorial or act of remembrance. The hymns of the

Wesleys show that this is too simple a dichotomy, and in recent years it has been widely said in ecumenical circles that agreement on the vexed question of Eucharistic sacrifice is in sight. Thus just as in the practice of weekly communion, so in the formulation of a doctrine of Eucharistic sacrifice which combines "Catholic" and Protestant elements, the Wesleys can be shown to have anticipated the modern trend. In indicating, however, the nature of this agreement, I must sound also a note of caution, for the reconciliation of "Catholic" and Protestant elements is unfortunately not yet as complete as some ecumenical enthusiasts would have us believe, though undoubtedly it is far more complete than many who are still entrenched in old controversies would suppose.

That the death of Christ may be described in sacrificial categories seems beyond dispute. A modern Methodist, Vincent Taylor, has shown the richness of New Testament teaching on this point. There are of course theories of the atonement other than the sacrificial; there are the Abelardian, the penal, the *Christus Victor* theories. Wherever we start, however, we ought surely to make some use of the sacrificial categories which are used by the New Testament itself—and not only Hebrews or Paul but also the synoptic Gospels. They are not the only categories—some would say not the chief categories—which the New Testament uses, but they are sufficiently prominent to make it permissible for us to use them. Of course problems arise about their interpretation and possible demythologization, but that is true of almost all the New Testament categories. It is also obvious that the New Testament refers not only to the sacrificial death of Christ but also to the sacrifice of praise and the sacrifice of ourselves and to priesthood, the high priesthood of Christ and the royal priesthood of God's people.

When we ask, however, whether in some sense a sacrificial character attaches to the Lord's Supper, which is the memorial of his sacrificial death, the New Testament gives no plain answer, though we note that in First Corinthians Paul, admittedly for a particular purpose, draws an analogy between the Lord's Supper and pagan sacrifices and sees the Supper as a participation (*koinonia*) in the

Body and Blood of Christ (I Cor. 10:16), so that some scholars speak of the Lord's Supper as a sharing in Christ's sacrifice. The amplification of this idea is to be found in the Fathers, and there are three main types of theory which we may attribute respectively to Irenaeus, Cyprian, and Augustine. Wesley, in his emphasis on the passion, most closely resembles Cyprian.

Let us turn to Wesley himself. Our exposition will be based on *Hymns on the Lord's Supper* by John Wesley and Charles Wesley. It is sometimes contended that this doctrine springs from Charles rather than John, but this seems to be a somewhat *a priori* judgment about what John is likely to have held. John was surely too careful a man to allow his name to be used in connection with doctrines which he did not approve. Before the hymns there is a preface "The Christian Sacrament and Sacrifice," extracted from Dr. Brevint.[2] The hymns are divided into sections, each of which has a heading; the wording of the headings closely corresponds to that of the section headings in Brevint, who was a Caroline divine. In order to put the hymns on sacrifice into their context I shall deal briefly with all the sections. The hymns themselves are often almost a paraphrase of Brevint.

The first of the sections in *Hymns on the Lord's Supper* is headed "As it is a Memorial of the Sufferings and Death of Christ." The word "memorial," *anamnesis,* has been much discussed in recent ecumenical theology. The view has been expressed by Professor Jeremias and others that the words in I Cor. 11:24 usually translated "this do in remembrance of me" should be translated "this do to remind God of me." It is still in dispute whether this is linguistically sound, but the objection that it is improper for us to

[2] The hymns and the preface are most conveniently accessible in J. Ernest Rattenbury, *The Eucharistic Hymns of John and Charles Wesley* (London: The Epworth Press 1948), which contains within itself the whole book. In citing the hymns, I give the numbers as in the Wesleys and in Rattenbury. Some of the hymns are of course in the hymnbooks in common use. I have followed the original text, but with some modernization of spelling and punctuation. Hymns which are not found in *Hymns on the Lord's Supper* I have cited from *The Methodist Hymn-Book* (London, 1933), and these numbers are prefixed by *M.H.B.*

remind God of anything would have found no echo in the Wesleys, for in the hymn "Lamb of God, whose bleeding love We thus recall to mind" (20) each verse ends:

> O remember *Calvary*
> And bid us go in peace.

Whatever may be thought of this theory, we may accept the view widely held in ecumenical circles that *anamnesis* is more than a psychological recollecting and is a rather a dynamic re-calling. The linguistic evidence for this is not always clearly stated, but it seems to be in harmony with biblical modes of thought. The Wesleys, however, were rather prone to use the phrases "recall to mind" and "call to mind," which do not altogether support this view.

The second section is headed "As it is a Sign and a Means of Grace." I pause here only to note the hymn "Come, Holy Ghost, Thine influence shed" (72). When it was the fashion to think that the great prayer of the Eucharist should have an epiclesis in the Eastern style, this hymn was hailed by liturgically minded Methodists as evidence that the Wesleys were pioneers in the recognition of this need. But now that fuller understanding of the Jewish method of consecration by thanksgiving has drawn attention again away from the epiclesis, this hymn has fallen into the background once more.

The third section "The Sacrament a Pledge of Heaven" shows the Wesleys to be pioneers of what is now called "realized eschatology." It thus throws an indirect light on the question of sacrifice. At the Lord's Supper the barriers of time are in some sense, though not literally, transcended. Thus we are not yet in heaven, but we have an earnest of the messianic feast. We shall see in a moment that this is true also of the past. We are not literally taken back to Calvary, but in some sense we *are* taken back there.

We now come to the controversial fourth section, "The Holy Eucharist as it implies a Sacrifice," which begins with the great hymn "Victim divine" (116). The Wesleys never for a moment doubted that the sacrifice of Calvary, the one oblation once offered, was unique and unrepeatable. But, on their view, in remembering this, we plead it or present it, as what Brevint called a "commemorative sacrifice"; that is, we spread it before the Father as the only ground of all our hope. I illustrate this from a hymn that is not well known, "All hail, Redeemer of mankind" (124). In the following passage we shall observe first the entirely satisfactory evangelical emphasis on the sufficiency of Christ's redeeming work and then the reference to our presenting it.

Angels and Men might strive in vain,
They could not add the smallest Grain
  T' augment thy Death's atoning Power,
The Sacrifice is all-compleate,
The Death Thou never canst repeat,
  Once offer'd up to die no more.

Yet may we celebrate below,
And daily thus Thine Offering shew
  Expos'd before thy Father's Eyes;
In this tremendous mystery
Present Thee bleeding on the Tree,
  Our everlasting Sacrifice.

Such language is not always acceptable to the modern evangelical; yet he will cheerfully sing John Wesley's somewhat unrhythmical translation of Zinzendorf (*M.H.B.* 370).

Even then this shall be all my plea—
Jesus hath lived, hath died for me!

In fact, however, it must be admitted that the Wesleys went beyond this. Thus the second stanza of "O God of our forefathers, hear" (125) almost anticipates the hymn "And now, O Father, mindful of the love" (*M.H.B.* 759) by William Bright, an Anglo-Catholic. The Wesleys wrote:

With solemn faith we offer up,
And spread before Thy glorious eyes
That only ground of all our hope,
That precious bleeding Sacrifice,
Which brings Thy grace on sinners down,
And perfects all our souls in one. (125.)

It is in such hymns that the Wesleys come near to Cyprian, who wrote "The passion of the Lord is the sacrifice which we offer" (*passio est enim Domini sacrificium quod offerimus*) (Ep. lxiii. 17). This is a welcome relief from those modern expositions of the Eucharist which so follow what Irenaeus said about its being an offering of the first fruits of creation, a kind of harvest festival, that they make no mention at all of the passion of the Lord. The reference to the passion is absolutely right, but I should not myself defend the use of the word "offer" either by Cyprian or by the Wesleys, though I can see that it is easily reached from such words as "plead" and "present."

This raises, however, the larger question, How did the Wesleys conceive of the present activity of Christ? Is he, in their view, being slain afresh; is he offering himself; is he sitting on the right hand of the Father; or what? We need to digress from the particular section which we were considering and ask this question about the writings of the Wesleys generally. There is no doubt that he is conceived of as standing before the throne of the Father to plead for us. So in "Entered the holy place above" (*M.H.B.* 232) one verse ends:

He pleads His passion on the tree,
He shows Himself to God for me.

And the next begins: "Before the throne my Saviour stands." Some have objected to such descriptions on the ground that the Bible speaks rather of Jesus as having taken his seat in triumph at the right hand of the Father. Of course Charles Wesley wrote in that way also; thus in "Rejoice, the Lord is King!" (*M.H.B.* 247) we read:

When He had purged our stains,
He took His seat above.

In these two descriptions, that he stands to plead and that he sits in triumph, the metaphors are indeed inconsistent, but there is no inconsistency between the two spiritual states which they represent.[3] This truth can be equally well expressed by saying that he pleads from the throne.[4]

There is, however, scriptural warrant for the disputed phrase. Christ is said to have entered heaven "now to appear in the presence of God on our behalf" (Heb. 9:24). There is also warrant for the word "standing" in "a Lamb standing, as . . . slain" (Rev. 5:6). That "as" is often found in the Wesleys. So in "Victim divine" (116):

Thou standest in the holiest place,
As now for guilty sinners slain.

And in "God of my salvation, hear" (*M.H.B.* 365):

Standing now as newly slain,
To Thee I lift mine eye.

Often this thought is expressed in vivid metaphors. In "O Thou eternal Victim, slain" (5) we have:

Thy offering still continues new,
Thy vesture keeps its bloody hue.

Again, In "Father, let the sinner go" (122) we have:

Still, O God, the blood is warm,
Cover'd with the blood we are.

A more theological account is given in a hymn which begins thus:

[3] I have heard a sentence to this effect; it was said to have come from the Archbishop of Canterbury (Dr. A. M. Ramsey), but I do not know the exact source.

[4] Cf. B. F. Westcott, *The Epistle to the Hebrews* (London, 1889), p. 230.

He dies, as now for us He dies!
That all-sufficient sacrifice
Subsists, eternal as the Lamb,
In every time and place the same;
To all alike it co-extends,
Its saving virtue never ends. (140.)

Apart from passages where the Wesleys regarded themselves, by a kind of poetic use of the historic present, as being present during Christ's passion or at the moment of his death or, indeed, of his resurrection, the dominant thought is that Christ's atoning death is as though it had just happened. The idea that the blood still flows is a way of saying that the death is still efficacious. Many ideas may be connected with this—the idea that in every generation a man must celebrate the passover "as if he came forth himself out of Egypt" [5] and the whole conception of annual commemoration and of liturgical time ("Christ the Lord is risen today"), the Pauline conception of dying and rising with Christ, Platonic notions of eternity, and so on, themes too large for investigation here.

We must regretfully admit that this way of transcending the categories of time sometimes led the Wesleys to speak of Christ still offering himself; so in "Thou Lamb that suffer'st on the Tree" (117) we have the line: "Still offer'st up Thyself to God." This goes beyond the scriptural notion that Christ still pleads, and the transition from Christ's pleading to Christ's offering resembles the transition which we noticed earlier from our pleading to our offering. In that earlier instance, however, there was more than an error about time, for there never was a time when we offered Christ, whereas the statement that Christ offers himself is unscriptural only as regards its tense.

These unscriptural expressions have led to some discussion of the relation of the Wesleys' view to the Roman view. There can be no doubt that in their stress on the uniqueness of the sacrifice of Calvary they repudiated the Roman view as popularly conceived. But a whole host of Anglican apologists, notably Bishop F. C. N.

[5] *Mishnah,* Pes. 10.5. I owe this reference to my colleague, the Rev. H. J. Cook.

Hicks in his book *The Fullness of Sacrifice,* have contended that, while we should reject distorted views based on medieval conceptions of sacrifice, we may well accept the true doctrine of Eucharistic sacrifice which, they contend, is common to true Romanism and true Anglicanism. Authors of this school may perhaps wish to include the Wesleys in their synthesis. This view goes somewhat as follows: The essence of sacrifice is not the slaying and death of the victim; these are only a preliminary stage which, in the case of Christ, is indeed concluded. Further stages are the oblation and the sacrificial meal. The oblation continues as Christ offers himself continually and eternally on the heavenly altar and we offer him continually in our Eucharists, and the sacrificial meal continues, as it were dispersedly, in the Church's Eucharists. Thus, on this view, we are neither commemorating a past sacrifice nor repeating it (a pair of false alternatives between which at the time of the Reformation men unfortunately thought they must choose). We are quite literally engaged still in the concluding stages of the one and original sacrifice.

This view, like some expressions of the Wesleys, disregards the scriptural statement that where there is remission of sins "there is no longer any offering for sin" (Heb. 10:18), but it does so much more flagrantly than the Wesleys did. The Wesleys did not regard themselves as present at a later stage of the one sacrifice, that stage being an essential part of the process, as Bishop Hicks affirmed; they did, indeed, emphasize the heavenly intercession of Christ, which is perfectly scriptural, but their main stress was on the cross itself, the only stage of the sacrifice proper. Their occasional use of unscriptural expressions arose partly from the vivid devotion which led them to feel that they were present at it and partly from the theological desire to make clear the fact that it is still potent and thus to emphasize our dependence on it.

The peace which Bishop Hicks and others thought they had established between conflicting views of this question was in any case shattered in 1960 by Father Francis Clark, S. J., in *Eucharistic Sacrifice and the Reformation;* he contended that the Roman doctrine was uncompromisingly the same throughout, that the alleged medieval distortions are a figment, and that the Reformers knew perfectly well what they were doing in rejecting the whole Roman doctrine of the sacrifice of the Mass; from their own point of view the Reformers were acting rightly. Moreover, the focal point of sacrifice is indeed the slaying and death of the victim, as Romans and evangelicals have alike asserted. This book has thus disturbed an ecumenical *rapprochement* which had appealed to many moderates, and this has brought undisguised satisfaction to the more extreme evangelicals who had always been suspicious of this tendency. It is too early to say whether this book will command the general approval of critical opinion, and so for the moment the controversy rests there. It may well be true that Roman and Protestant opinions on this point are sharply opposed; after all, this is what Brevint and the Wesleys themselves believed, in company with the great mass of opinion, both Protestant and Roman, down the centuries. The Wesleys clearly intended to be on the Protestant side, as for the most part they unmistakably showed. For our purposes, however, it is not really necessary to determine what is the authentic Roman doctrine. If—despite Fr. Clark—it should ultimately emerge that the Roman position does not diverge from scripture as much as some Protestant polemical writing has made it appear to do, we ought to be eager to recognize the fact; what matters now is that the views of the Wesleys, including their slight divergence from scripture, should be made clear.

We may sum up these views by again saying that they strongly emphasized our utter dependence on the unique sacrifice of Christ. Calvary is the atoning or propitiatory sacrifice; the sacrament of the Lord's Supper is a commemorative or Eucharistic sacrifice, part of the "sacrifice of praise" (Heb. 13:15) of which scripture speaks. It is a *sacrificium* which is primarily *beneficium*. They linked the sacrifice of Calvary with the heavenly intercession of Christ which is based upon it, a doctrine which some evangelicals have neglected. The series of vivid metaphors which they employed to show that Christ's death retains its efficacy or that we may view it as though it had just happened is a rich contribution to the treasury of Eucharistic devotion. Never do they assert that the Eucharist *is* an atoning sacrifice, but, to return to the careful heading of the section which we have been considering, "it implies a Sacrifice."

The fifth section is headed "Concerning the Sacrifice of our Persons." There is very little here of the idea of Irenaeus that we offer the bread and wine as the first fruits of creation or of that of Augustine (*Sermon* 229) that as members of the Body of Christ *we* are on the table and in the cup. It is sometimes said today that, whereas the Roman doctrine is that we offer Christ, the Protestant doctrine is that Christ offers us, though actually the latter is no more a scriptural expression than the former. It is also said that we are presented to God and acceptable to him through our incorporation in the Body of Christ, and this is well expressed in a hymn, albeit an Anglo-Catholic hymn, to which reference has already been made, "And now, O Father, mindful of the love" (*M.H.B.* 759) in the line "And only look on us as found in Him." The Wesleys mostly express these truths in other ways; they speak of our self-oblation being joined to or mixed with that of Christ. They are fond of the notion of Christ as the Head; the correlative term, however, is not usually "body," but "members," and this does not lead to a strong theology of incorporation. The following lines from "See where our great High-Priest" (129) have not many parallels:

> With Him, the Corner-stone,
> The living stones conjoin;
> Christ and His church are one,
> One body and one vine.

According to the Wesleys Christ does not primarily offer us; he offered (and sometimes they say he offers) himself, and the Eucharist is spoken of in sacrificial terms primarily because it "implies" that sacrifice.

The sixth heading is simply "After the Sacrament." The content of the section is largely praise, for the previous section had dealt with self-oblation. It is perhaps too much to see in this a comment on the highly controversial question of the position of the prayer of oblation, which John Wesley, in fact, made no attempt to move.

When we come then to compare the Wesleys' views on Eucharistic sacrifice with those now common in the ecumenical movement we find an almost complete absence of the views derived from Irenaeus and Augustine which are now so common. These views, in my judgment, have until recently been accepted somewhat uncritically, but the warnings now sounded against what is called "offertory-theology" show a welcome hesitation and the beginnings of a reaction, at least as regards Irenaeus. Methodism has not moved in this direction and will not need to retrace its steps. But this comforting thought should not exempt us from asking whether there is not here some measure of truth of which we should be aware.

Our positive contribution lies in the somewhat Cyprianic doctrine of sacrifice to be found in the Wesleys. This has not been fully maintained in Methodism, and it is to this day probably more congenial to many non-Methodists than it is to us. The reason for our caution lies in the occasional use of expressions which go beyond a sound biblical theology, and we may well deplore the rather cavalier way in which some non-Methodist writers sweep aside evangelical objections to such phrases. Yet we are surely much to blame if, going beyond necessary caution, we blindly neglect the whole rich doctrine of the high-priesthood and heavenly intercession of Christ in their bearing on the Eucharist. When all is said, the Wesleys produced a doctrine far richer than that of most other writers, far richer than that of most of their successors. Their doctrine holds out at least some hope of reconciling so-called "catholic" and evangelical views. They deserve in this, as in much else, to be hailed as ecumenical pioneers. Indeed the more discerning spirits of the ecumenical movement have already paid them tribute, and we should hasten to draw the attention of liturgists and systematic theologians in this direction.

Only brief consideration need be given to the other doctrinal topic, the real presence. This has been the classic field of Eucharistic controversy—especially between Lutherans and Calvinists. Attempts have been made to classify the Wesleys in the traditional categories, as virtualists, dynamic receptionists, and so on. Their own comment, in "O the depth of love Divine" (57) was:

> Who shall say how bread and wine
> God into man conveys!

But a theology which transcends the bounds of time to some extent transcends this problem. If we are in some sense in the heavenly places or at Calvary, then clearly Christ is present. The Eucharist is the making present in time of the once-for-all sacrificial *act* of Christ. We are to ascribe to the humanity of Christ a time-universalization in contrast to a space-localization. Real presence is in an action rather than in a substance. Thus in Hebrew thought "the thing" is always "the thing done"; space is produced by event. In these last few sentences I have been quoting a liturgist of another communion who is himself in part quoting others;[6] and I venture to suggest that the Wesleys by their interest in the question of sacrifice and their comparative neglect of static and local doctrines of the real presence have to some extent anticipated this insight, or rather anticipated the revival of it, for it is itself biblical and patristic. The notion of "time-universalization" has its dangers, as we have seen, but it is nevertheless a very fruitful insight.

In the doctrinal part of this discussion I have sought to throw the spotlight on the relation of the Wesleys to two major fields of controversy about the Lord's Supper rather than to give a general exposition of the doctrine. Such an exposition would contain references to other familiar truths such as that the Lord's Supper is a meal of fellowship with the saints on earth and the saints in heaven. If my contentions are true, however, then the Wesleys in their sac-

[6] The reference is to T. O. Wedel in *The Liturgical Renewal of the Church*, edited by Massey H. Shepherd, Jr. (New York: Oxford University Press, 1960), pp. 6, 11.

ramental practice and in their carefully balanced sacramental doctrine, as much as in their evangelical practice and emphasis, have much to teach the universal Church—much that, rightly understood, might yet serve to reconcile many, if not all, the tensions within Christendom. To the ecumenical movement we may yet hope to contribute it, but first we must ourselves possess our possessions and seek to enter, not only academically but also devotionally, into their spirit.

9

The Discipline of Life in Early Methodism Through Preaching and Other Means of Grace

GERALD O. McCULLOH

The Methodist movement, from its beginnings, has been concerned with the discipline and nurture which are essential to the new life given through grace by faith. Our task today is to discover the necessary engagements of the ongoing life of those who have become convinced of the truth of the gospel and who in penitence receive the forgiveness of their sins and seek to lead a new life following the commandments of God.

What was the nature and purpose of discipline for Wesley and the early Methodists? How was it structured, and how was it engendered and enforced through preaching and the means of grace? Wesley, in responding to an inquiry from the Vicar of Shoreham (1748) concerning the "people called Methodists," said that "they had no previous design or plan at all; but everything arose just as the occasion offered. They saw or felt some impending or pressing evil, or some good end necessary to be pursued. And many times they fell unawares on the very thing which secured the good, or removed the evil." [1] This would seem to be the very opposite of discipline and order in the Christian life. Such an accidental and purely planless approach to the life of Christian belief and behavior hardly describes and surely does not account for the central and original attention which Wesley and his followers gave to the forms and the fact of discipline in devotion and action in the rise of the Methodist movement. Methodism arose, as Albert Outler correctly calls to our attention in the opening chapter, as an enterprise in evangelical mission, with the central attention focused upon witness, discipline, and nurture.

As Wesley had bound himself to the demands of a rigorous pattern of devotional discipline, so he called upon all who would be made perfect in love to give themselves to the daily discipline of obedience. "All who expect to be sanctified at all," he wrote in a letter to Dorothy Furly, August 19, 1759, "expect to be sanctified by faith. But meantime they know that faith will not be given but to them that obey."

This implied more than a haphazard experimentalism. It is the recognition of one of the grounds of growth in faith and grace through obedience. Here is the real basis of the kind of adherence to the forms of discipline which both elicited the epithet "Methodist" and gave a characteristic image to the people who took their religion in dead earnest. Preaching and discipline were the bench marks of the early Methodist movement. We have not left off preaching, but what has become of our discipline?

The importance of our inquiry into the historic meaning of "the discipline of life" in our tradition does not stem from any failure to retain the term "discipline." It is rather that we have permitted the term "discipline" and its connotation to move into an almost purely institutional and legal realm. We have seen our "disciplines" disappear with the passing of the class meeting and other means of

[1] "A Plain Account of the People Called Methodists."

grace, either in fact or in form, from their original intention and usage.

The development of the term "discipline" in Methodist parlance discloses various levels of reference. In Wesley's own early life and usage it meant the acceptance of a pattern or order in the practice and exercises of the devotional life. As the Methodist movement took form and spread it became apparent that the increasing numbers of persons must be organized into societies and classes in order to provide spiritual leadership and discipline for the members. Both instruction and oversight in matters spiritual and moral were included in the administration of discipline, which was the responsibility of the leader. Continuance of membership in the society was contingent upon the individual member's obedience to the "rules," which became the instruments whereby the organization maintained a consistency of life and behavior on the part of its members.

With the convening of conferences the term "discipline" came to be used for the ordered agenda of the conference sessions. The work of the conference was carried on by asking and answering questions regarding the organizational life and development of the movement. Step by step "discipline" has passed over into a highly legal and constitutional denotation until in the "Glossary" in the *Discipline* of The Methodist Church in the United States (1960), it is said to mean, "The official and published statement of the Constitution and laws of The Methodist Church, its rules of organization and procedure, the description of administrative agencies and their functions, and the Ritual." [2]

However, in the Episcopal Greetings which form the introduction to the same volume, there is a clear recognition of the earlier meaning and importance of discipline in Methodism. Discipline, it is noted, was instrumental to, as well as a record of, "the successive stages of spiritual insight attained by Methodists under the grace of Christ." [3] The class meeting "soon revealed its fitness for religious

[2] Nashville: The Methodist Publishing House, 1960, p. 725.
[3] *Ibid.*, p. 1.

nurture and took that work as its chief aim." [4] The episcopal statement then calls the reader to share in an attitude toward the organizational life of the church which is designed to recover the instrumentality of the church in the work of the Holy Spirit and the life of grace. "We reverently insist that a fundamental aim of Methodism is to make her organization an instrument for the development of spiritual life. . . . We do now express the faith and hope that the prayerful observance of the spiritual intent of the *Discipline* may be to the people called Methodists a veritable means of grace." [5] In a period when the church has become so preoccupied with the institutional demands of her organization and program that she is in danger of becoming just another circle of operation for "the organization man," or with definition to the point where we may be in danger of a new "Gnosticism," a call to a recovery of the discipline of life may not be out of place, and if heeded could result in a reopening of the lives of Methodists and the life of the church to the guidance and power of the Holy Spirit. Henry Carter, in *The Methodist Heritage,* notes the results of discipline in early Methodism in these words: "The quality of fellowship in the Methodist class-meetings and the effectiveness of Methodist discipline in the lifetime of the Wesleys upheld the apostolic teaching, and went far to ensure that the profession of the individual was tested by collective Christian experience." [6] Here was a means of strengthening the experience of community among Christians under the disclosing light of the gospel.

The following review of the development of the discipline of life in the life of John Wesley and the early Methodist societies is undertaken with the hope that in the recovery of discipline we may be led onward in the expectation and realization of the purity of life and the fullness of holy love which Wesley saw to be the responsibility which follows upon receiving the gift of forgiveness and justification. To this end the gathering of the congregation of faithful men and women, the preaching of the Word of the

[4] *Ibid.*
[5] *Ibid.,* pp. 1-2.
[6] Nashville: Abingdon-Cokesbury Press, 1951, p. 66.

gospel, the administration of the sacraments and the employment of the historic means of grace, may find their rightful instrumentality, and the church may achieve a new and unifying power unto man's salvation. To the first level of meaning of "discipline" in the Methodist movement we shall direct our attention, with the earnest desire that a recovery of discipline in these terms may serve to correct and displace ecclesiastical legalism, and to cleanse the church anew for her rightful role in the salvation of man and society.

Happy the souls to Jesus joined,
And saved by grace alone;
Walking in all his ways, they find
Their heaven on earth begun.

The Church triumphant in thy love,
Their mighty joys we know:
They sing the Lamb in hymns above,
And we in hymns below.

. . . .

The holy to the holiest leads,
And thence our spirits rise;
For he that in thy statutes treads
Shall meet thee in the skies.

In these lines from Charles Wesley's hymn "The Kingdoms One" the emphasis upon salvation as a gift of grace and the responsibility of man through the Holy Spirit to walk in Christ's ways are placed together in a way which was characteristic of John Wesley's conjoining of faith and works. It is in and through the church that man is enjoined to tread in the divine statutes under the vocation to holiness and the hope of heaven.

Personal Discipline of John Wesley

The practice of personal discipline was instilled early in the life of the founder of Methodism. Of the home experience in the rectory at Epworth, Carter observed: "The quality and ordering of the family life made deep and lasting impression on the sons and daughters of the household. Not only was the home religious and scholarly, but also firmly disciplined." [7] The Lord's prayer, the collects, the catechism, portions of the scripture, and a weekly conference period with Susanna, their mother and mentor, were the earliest of the regular devotional means within the Wesley family. To these were added, when an appropriate age was reached, attendance upon the offices and services of the church, in worship, preaching, and the holy communion.

When the Wesley sons proceeded to Oxford they found a new urgency to disciplined attention to devotional practice. Charles wrote to John during a period of his absence from Oxford that "Christ Church is certainly the worst place in the world to begin a reformation in. A man stands a fair chance of being laughed out of his religion at his first setting out, in a place where 'tis scandalous to have any at all." [8] Yet it was here that these young men of disciplined purpose and practice formed "The Holy Club" and were thereupon derisively called "Methodists," because of the precise and methodical manner of their lives as well as of their studies and formal religious observance. As John recorded his development in his *Journal,* he traced the beginning of his rigorous ordering of every hour to an advice given by Jeremy Taylor in his *Rules for Holy Living and Holy Dying.* The *Imitation of Christ* and Law's *Serious Call to a Devout and Holy Life* also entered determinatively into Wesley's experience during the Oxford days. It is suggested in a description of the Oxford Methodists attributed to William Law:

> That this society think themselves obliged in all particulars to live up to the law of the gospel. That the *Rule* they have set themselves is not that of their own inventions but the Holy Scriptures, and the orders and injunctions of the Church, and that not as they perversely construe and misinterpret them, but as they find them in the holy canon. That, pursuant to these, they have resolved to observe with strictness not only all

[7] *Op. cit.,* p. 16.

[8] Quoted in Frank Baker, *Charles Wesley as Revealed by His Letters* (Wesley Historical Society Lectures, No. 14; London: The Epworth Press, 1948), p. 11.

the duties of the Christian religion according to their baptismal engagements, but the fasts, the prayers, and sacraments of the Church; to receive the blessed Communion as often as there is opportunity; and to do all the good they can, in visiting the sick, the poor, the prisoners, etc., knowing these to be the great articles on which they are to be tried at the last day; and in all things to keep themselves unspotted from the world. . . . These are the *Rules,* this the *Method,* they have chosen to live by.[9]

The purpose of this discipline, Wesley wrote to Richard Morgan, January 15, 1734, was to achieve "a constant ruling habit of soul, a renewal of our minds in the image of God, a recovery of the divine likeness, a still-increasing conformity of heart and life to the pattern of our most holy Redeemer." He was seeking holiness, Christian perfection. Whatever he knew to be hurtful or evil, he eschewed. Whatever he knew to do him good he resolutely embraced. The sermon "On The Duty of Constant Communion" records his finding together in the grace given through the Lord's Supper the strength to perform his duty and the leading of the soul on to perfection.

The disciplines of Oxford were carried to Georgia and, after Wesley's return to England, into the ordering of his life's further quest. The absence of a "sure trust and confidence in God," which he sensed as a lack of faith, was not, he discovered, to be relieved by the energetic, if not frenzied, application of himself to the discipline of doing good. His awareness of the necessity for complete self-surrender and total trust deepened until, under the guidance of the Moravians and the witness of the spirit in his Aldersgate hour, the justification for which he longed was given through faith with assurance. He saw his former striving to be "fighting continually, but not conquering." He had been "striving with, not freed from, sin." When he came to seek faith as an instantaneous gift of grace, by renouncing all dependence upon

[9] "The Oxford Methodists," quoted by Umphrey Lee, *John Wesley and Modern Religion* (Nashville: Cokesbury Press, 1936), pp. 214-15.

his own works of righteousness, he found it. He did so "by adding to the constant use of all the other means of grace, continual prayer for this very thing, justifying, saving faith, a full reliance on the blood of Christ for *me;* a trust in Him, as *my* Christ, as *my* sole justification, sanctification and redemption." [10] The assurance of justification through faith alone was experienced first at Aldersgate. The atonement, seen to be the sole and adequate ground of man's justification, was accepted in that moment as God's gracious gift. This legacy of the Reformation here entered into Wesley's life and preaching, never to be surrendered. George Croft Cell, noting the importance of the atonement in Wesley's preaching, said: "He was immovable in the belief that an objective atonement is the life principle of the Christian message and the all-inclusive differential of genuine Christianity." [11] Atonement remained for Wesley as the central issue between Deism and Christianity.

Yet the possession of this "*instantaneous* blessing" resulted in "rather an increase than a decrease of zeal for the whole work of God and every part of it." [12] For himself and all who entered into the life of the Methodist movement Wesley sought to enforce "the *gradual* work" of sanctification beyond the first fullness of forgiveness and justification. Not only must the guilt of sin be atoned and the sinner forgiven, the power of sin was to be broken and its roots completely destroyed; this by continuing growth in grace through the discipline of life by the power of the Spirit.

Reliance upon the grace of God was, for Wesley, not permitted to dull the edge of conscience nor to dim the eye of the soul to the imperious expectation of purity and perfect love. "I have found," said Wesley, "that even the precious doctrine of *Salvation by Faith* has need to be guarded with the utmost care or those who hear it will slight both inward and outward holiness." [13]

[10] *Journal* (May, 1738), "A Review of Life."

[11] *The Rediscovery of John Wesley* (New York: Henry Holt and Company, 1935), p. 338.

[12] Letter to Charles Wesley, June 27, 1766.

[13] Cited by Cell, *op. cit.,* 342.

Discipline in the Societies

The discipline of life, which Wesley found to be continuingly instrumental to growth in grace for himself, was bound upon those who came to him for counsel to the end that the image of God might be restored [14] and that man might be made perfect in love. He did not indulge in a puritanical resort to negations or self-justifying denials. There were, he commented, no hair-cloth shirts or bodily austerities. Neither was there any desire to achieve a pale and barren harmlessness, such as would elicit no negative reaction from fellow citizens or contemporaries. Nor were the Methodists to be content with the mere externals of doing good in works of piety and charity, nor with formal reliance on the established means of grace. Rather he insisted that those who came to him for guidance should seek "the mind that was in Christ," should desire earnestly to have the image of God stamped upon their hearts. The goal was "inward righteousness, attended with the peace of God; and 'joy in the Holy Ghost.' " [15] Discipline was regarded as instrumental to the fruits of faith. All who attached themselves to the movement were expected (1) to rejoice in God, (2) to walk as becomes the gospel, (3) to be fruitful in good works and evangelism, (4) to mutually strengthen one another in love, and (5) to share the expectation of entire sanctification. Obedience is useful "to provoke those who have peace with God to abound more in love and good works." [16]

The Objective of Discipline

Wesley regarded the methodical disciplines which he required of his converts as instrumental to growth in grace and godliness. The discipline, like the law of God, was not an end in itself. The end to be sought was final justification and glorification in heavenly

[14] See "The New Birth," *Sermons;* cf. Piette, *John Wesley in the Evolution of Protestantism,* p. 440.

[15] "A Plain Account of the People Called Methodists."

[16] "The Character of a Methodist."

bliss. Those who had been born again into new life, being justified by faith, yet faced the necessity of spiritual growth.

Discipline was not regarded as a merely human enterprise in pleasing God by good works after justification. It was itself a gift and means of grace received under the direction and dynamic of the Holy Spirit.

The objective of discipline was, as has been shown, the opening of the heart to the perfecting work of the spirit unto sanctification. The fulfillment of the demands of pure love and holiness was the moral counterpart and outcome of the new life which had been received through faith.

The "Rules" of Discipline

In his "Plain Account of the People Called Methodists," Wesley recounts the history of the establishing of "a society." He shows the purpose of the institution of the "Rules" to be for the discipline of those who "united themselves 'in order to pray together, to receive the word of exhortation, and to watch over one another in love, that they might help each other work out their salvation.' " In the life of the society many were strengthened in rejoicing unto God; "disorderly walkers" were detected, of whom some turned from the evil of their ways, and others were expelled from the fellowship. Wesley himself entered periodically ("at least once in three months") into conversation with the members of the early societies to inquire "whether they grew in grace and in the knowledge of our Lord Jesus Christ." This quarterly visitation and the "ticket" which was issued to the earnest and faithful provided a method of excluding the undisciplined member. For the members of the societies "the war [with temptation] was not over, as they had supposed; but they had still to wrestle both with flesh and blood, and with principalities and powers." The more earnest seekers were organized into "bands" for intimate mutual confession and strengthening.

The chains were broken, the bands were burst in sunder, and sin had no more dominion over them. Many were delivered from the temptations out of which, till then, they found no way to escape. They were built up in our most holy faith. They rejoiced in the Lord abundantly. They were strengthened in love, and more effectually provoked to abound in every good work.

In addition to the meetings of the societies and bands, there were the love feasts, the watch nights, the letter days, and the intimate and select company of the backsliders who, having found the way again, shared testimonies and confessions which were not to be repeated. There were rules for the leaders, the stewards, and the assistants. Special attention was paid to the sick and the indigent. Employment, loan funds, and gifts to the needy who were unable to work were expressions of the concern of all for each one in the fellowship.

The "Rules" of discipline were almost invariably threefold. The "Directions Given to the Band Societies, December 25, 1744" call attention to the supposition that all in the Band Society "have the faith that overcometh the world." This faith was to be expressed in works of obedience. Therefore all the members were admonished: (1) "carefully to abstain from all evil," (2) "zealously to maintain good works," and (3) "constantly to attend on all the ordinances of God." Under each heading a list of particulars makes the members' duty clear. The proscriptions of "needless ornaments, such as rings, ear-rings, necklaces, lace, ruffles"; and, "needless self-indulgence, such as taking snuff or tobacco, unless prescribed by a Physician," may seem overmeticulous. But the admonitions "to be at church and at the Lord's table every week," "to attend the ministry of the word every morning," "to use private prayer [and family prayer] every day," "to read the Scriptures, and meditate therein, at every vacant hour," and "to observe, as days of fasting and abstinence, all Fridays in the year," reflect the requirements of obedience to the divine ordinances and to the "Rules."

The Means of Grace

That the disciplines which we have been considering were regarded by Wesley to be "means of grace" is clearly shown in his question to the "Helpers" in the "Minutes of Several Conversations Between the Rev. Mr. Wesley and Others from the year 1744, to the year 1789":

. . . Do you use all the means of grace yourself, and enforce the use of them on all other persons?

They are either Instituted or Prudential:—

I. The *Instituted* are,

(1) Prayer; private, family, public . . . .

(2) Searching the Scriptures by,

(i) Reading . . . .

(ii) Meditating . . . .

(iii) Hearing . . . .

(3) The Lord's Supper . . . .

(4) Fasting . . . .

(5) Christian conference . . . .

II. *Prudential means* we may use either as common Christians, as Methodists, as Preachers, or as Assistants.

(1) As common Christians. What particular rules have you in order to grow in grace? What arts of holy living?

(2) As Methodists. Do you ever miss your class, or Band?

(3) As Preachers. Do you meet every society; also the Leaders and Bands, if any?

(4) As Assistants. . . . do you make a conscience of executing every part of [your office]?

Then follows an even stronger and more specific word of watching against the world, the devil, and self. Self-denial and temperance in both food and drink were urged. The closing question places the foregoing specific admonitions in their relation to divine grace. "Do you endeavor to set God always before you; to see his eye continually fixed upon you? Never can you use these means but a blessing will ensue. And the more you use them, the more will you grow in grace."

The instituted means were seen to center in the sacramental act of partaking of the Lord's Supper. Wesley held that this sacrament was ordained by God as a means to "preventing," "justifying," or "sanctifying" grace, according to the individual person's need. The sermons on "The Means of Grace" and "The Duty of Constant Communion" make it clear that obedience to God's ordinances is a mandate, not an option. "Because God bids, therefore I do." That the Lord's Supper was to be received through the offices of the church is the clearest evidence of his stand against individualism, enthusiasm, or antinomianism. Even the much disputed ordinations designed to provide discipline, order, and the sacraments for the Methodists in America were undertaken in the context of the usages within the historic Christian Church, not apart from it. "Let us never make light of going to church, either by word or deed." [17] There was to be no substitution of the Methodist services for the "Church Service." "When the Methodists leave the church, God will leave them." [18] Attracted as Wesley had been to the Moravians he could not accept their rejection of the ordinances and offices of the church. "No works, no law, no commandments," he called the wellspring of the great error of the Moravians. "The imagination that faith supersedes holiness is the marrow of antinomianism." [19] Obedience to the "law of God" Wesley likewise saw to be the necessary counter emphasis to the Solfidianism of the Lutheran doctrine as he knew it. Faith in Christ no more delivers man from obedience to the law than it delivers him from holiness and heaven. Wesley's confidence in the meeting of persons together at fixed times for confession and prayer stemmed from his conviction that such Christian conference was a part of the order of God's law. "How dare any man deny this to be (as to the substance of it) a means of grace, ordained by God? Unless he will affirm (with Luther in the fury of his Solfidianism) that St. James' Epistle is an epistle of straw." [20] Thus discipline, ecclesiastical and moral, appears as a responsibility of man in obedience to the spirit's leading, enabling, and sanctifying power. Apart from the disciplined life the faith which is given in life-renewing power at justification dies.

[17] "Minutes of Several Conversations."
[18] *Ibid.*
[19] *Journal,* VII, 316 f (Cf. *Compend,* 167).
[20] *Journal,* April 4, 1739.

Preaching

Preaching was not included in the lists of the "means of grace" which have been cited. Yet preaching was an essential instrumentality for awakening sinners and for guiding the lives of the reborn.

The importance of preaching as a distinguishing mark of Wesley's own work and of the Wesleyan movement can hardly be overestimated. Records and journals of the early Methodist leaders abound in references to preaching in homes, in the fields, in meetinghouses, in prisons, and in the shadow of the gallows at public hangings. One statistically minded researcher has estimated that John Wesley himself "preached no less than 52,400 times between 1738, when he returned from Georgia, and 1791, when he preached his last sermon eight days before he died." [21] So closely was preaching associated with the ministers who were first called "Methodist" that David C. Shipley, in a paper on "The Ministry in Methodism in the Eighteenth Century," could say graphically that "History has united, genetically, the terms 'Methodist and preacher.' " [22] The Methodist preachers, clergymen and laymen alike, were those whom the spirit of God "called" in a special way to proclaim "remission of sins through Jesus Christ." [23] It will be remembered that Wesley admonished his preachers to "Preach abroad as much as possible. . . . Try every town and village." [24] This he gave as the answer to the question, "What can be done to increase the work of God . . . ?"

The method of preaching which Wesley recommended was fourfold: " (1.) To invite. (2.) To convince. (3.) To offer Christ. (4.) To build up." [25] Its function is thus seen to be to bring sinners to a conviction of their lost state and to offer them Christ and his salvation. Wesley told his preachers not to preach too much of the

[21] Oscar Sherwin, *John Wesley, Friend of the People* (New York: Twayne Publishers, Inc., 1961), p. 71.

[22] *The Ministry in the Methodist Heritage,* edited by Gerald O. McCulloh (Nashville: Board of Education of The Methodist Church, 1960), p. 15.

[23] John Wesley, letter to the Lord Bishop of London, June 11, 1747.

[24] "Minutes of Several Conversations."

[25] *Ibid.*

wrath, but much of the love of God.[26] Preaching did not stop there, however. Wesley, it has been suggested, was not an evangelist in the meaning which that term has later acquired. He did not preach without building up the lives of his converts through relating them to the offices of the church and the discipline of life in the societies. Wesley warned against "preaching Christ" as a fond alternative to "practical preaching." In the sense in which he recommended it as a method of building up the hearers, preaching itself was a part of the discipline. He advised that sermons deal expressly with "Sabbath-breaking, dram-drinking, evil-speaking, unprofitable conversation, lightness, expensiveness or gaiety of apparel, and contracting debts without due care to discharge them." [27] Preaching was further a means of guarding the hearers against errors in doctrine and the deadliness of formality either in worship or good works. Wesley's own sermons, such as "The Original Nature, Property, and Use of the Law," "Self-Denial," "The Cure of Evil-speaking," "The Use of Money," "The Reformation of Manners," "The Danger of Riches," "On Dissipation," "On Public Diversions," and the like, show him to have acted on his own advices. On an occasion such as the preaching of "The Almost Christian" in Saint Mary's (Oxford), the reader can feel what must have been the rousing and cumulative indictment as the forms of godly observance customary in that celebrated church were declared to be "almost" but not "altogether" Christian. Then the invitation was offered the hearers to go on into love to God, love to neighbor, and to faith. He said:

> Are not many of you conscious, that you never came thus far; that you have not been even *almost a Christian;* that you have not come up to the standard of heathen honesty; at least, not to the form of Christian godliness?—Much less hath God seen sincerity in you, a real design of pleasing him in all things. You never so much as intended to devote all your words and works, your business, studies, diversions, to his glory.

The hearers were castigated. Yet in other sermons, such as "The

[26] "Minutes of Some Late Conversations Between the Rev. Mr. Wesleys and Others."

[27] "Minutes of Several Conversations."

Wilderness State" and "Heaviness Through Manifold Temptations," Wesley's mood was entirely different. He was tender and understanding. The loss of love, of faith, of joy, and of God by those who through sin have become lost in the wilderness, or through cumulative temptation in "numberless circumstances" have found their hearts heavy within them brought forth from the preacher a gentle but insistent affirmation of the forgiving love of God. To these there is the proffering anew of the life of love, and joy, and holiness through sanctifying grace. Wesley's preaching was designed to proclaim and interpret the gospel to the various needs of men for salvation.

Although preaching was unmentioned among "the means of grace," yet we must regard it as such in the uses to which it was put by Wesley and his preachers. In the preface to "Sermons on Several Occasions" he declared his intention to be:

> First, to guard those who are just setting their faces toward heaven, (and who, having little acquaintance with the things of God, are the more liable to be turned out of the way,) from formality, from mere outside religion, which has almost driven heart-religion out of the world; and, Secondly, to warn those who know the religion of the heart, the faith which worketh by love, lest at any time they make void the law through faith, and so fall back into the snare of the devil.

Preaching, so regarded, was instrumental to growth in knowledge and grace, a discipline of the life wherein desire is fixed upon perfection in obedience and love to God.

Preaching was seen to have its limitations. It was not a "harangue unto holiness" without the involvement of the hearers in the other practices of discipline. Wesley suggests that persons awakened by preaching alone are only half awake. "I determine," he wrote in his *Journal,* "by the grace of God, not to strike one stroke in any place where I cannot follow the blow." (March 12, 1743.) He did not, as did George Whitefield, the evangelist, merely "preach and hope for the best." Organization of societies, supervision of group discipline, and pastoral visitation were required of the Methodist preacher. Of the inadequacy of preaching alone Wesley wrote in his *Journal:*

> I reached Colcester. I found the society had decreased . . . and yet they had had full as good preachers. But that is not sufficient. By repeated experiments we learn that, though a man preach like an angel, he will neither collect nor preserve a society which is collected, without visiting them from house to house. (December 27, 29, 1758.)

The Methodist preacher had to be more than a preacher. It was demanded of him that he "watch over souls, as he that must give account." [28] The account included the overseeing of the daily walk in obedience, in righteousness, in faith, and in holy love.

Nearly all that has been said here would find its parallel in the annals of the American Methodist societies. Thomas Coke and Francis Asbury, in their *Notes to the Discipline,* urged the establishment of the band societies in the new land. "There is nothing we know of," they said, "which so much quickens the soul to a desire and expectation of the perfect love of God as this." Then after giving the "rules" of discipline they added, "Thus does our economy . . . tend to raise the members of our Society from one degree of grace to another." [29] Asbury set the pattern of American Methodism in his preaching, his organizing and disciplining of the societies, and his pastoral oversight of both preachers and people. One of his first acts in taking over the leadership of the society in New York was to "keep the door," admitting only the qualified members. Such an action made him unpopular with those who had become accustomed to laxity of discipline, but he would not surrender his determination to bring the Wesleyan rules to the societies in America. The purpose of the American Methodist circuit rider, though his distances were longer and his traveling terrain somewhat rougher than those of his British counterpart, was to

[28] "Minutes of Several Conversations."

[29] Cited by John Leland Peters, *Christian Perfection and American Methodism* (Nashville: Abingdon Press, 1956), p. 94.

"spread scriptural holiness throughout the land," and "to watch over souls, as he that must give account."

In the middle of the following century (1841) Bishop Elijah Hedding published a *Discourse on the Administration of Discipline,* which shows the continuing place of discipline in the American branch of the church. He traced the responsibilities of the bishop, the presiding elder, the preacher in charge, the local preacher, the class leader, and the lay member in the maintenance of the laws and observances of the Methodist order. He said:

> The great work of discipline is to instruct, educate, and govern the people, and thus help them on toward heaven: to restrain and keep them from evil, or warn, reprove, and reclaim them when they may have erred, or fallen into sin. To accomplish this, the pastor is to labour "publicly, and from house to house;" "to be instant in season, out of season; reprove, rebuke, exhort, with all long-suffering and doctrine." The sick, the aged, the bereaved and sorrowful, are to be visited, admonished, encouraged, and comforted, as their condition and wants may require. The youth and the children are to be the objects of the care of the faithful shepherd. To perform these important and benevolent duties, he must avail himself of all the helps under his control. His colleague is his assistant in this work, and has his portion of care and labours, as well as the preacher in charge. The local preachers are to be associated with the itinerants in these services.
>
> A minister is bound *to take heed to all the flock over which the Holy Ghost has made him an overseer.*[30]

Was this discipline a part of the work of the church or apart from it? This question serves to indicate the relation of this consideration to our general theme of "The Doctrine of the Church" and to point to a wider concern for an understanding of Methodism's part in the ecumenical movement. Does emphasis on this kind of discipline—particularly that of an intimate fellowship or band—tend to take its adherents out of the church, or does it prove to be an essential element in what the church can provide and must

[30] Reprint (Nashville: Southern Methodist Publishing House, 1861), pp. 39-40, 53.

in fact be? Neither the question nor its implication is new. In Wesley's words it was asked thus: "Is not this making a schism? Is not the joining these people together, gathering Churches out of Churches?" [31] His answer was given with something of the fire of an apologete. He acknowledged that it was gathering people out of buildings called churches, but it was not dividing Christians from Christians. It was providing Christian fellowship for the lonely, Christian joy for the wretched, and Christian strength for the weak. It was introducing the strong band of fellowship in place of the "rope of sand" which was the formal tie of the parish. "And the fruits of it have been peace, joy, love, and zeal for every good word and work." [32]

In utter realism Wesley confesses in another connection that he had feared that the disciplined and intimate fellowship of the Methodists would result in "a narrowness of spirit, a party zeal, . . . that miserable bigotry which makes many so unready to believe that there is any work of God but among ourselves." [33] He then went on to describe a part of the discipline itself which was designed to provide the safeguard.

> I thought it might help against this, frequently to read, to all who were willing to hear, the accounts I received from time to time of the work which God is carrying on in the earth, both in our own and other countries, not among us alone, but among those of various opinions and denominations. For this I allotted one evening in every month; and I find no cause to repent my labour. It is generally a time of strong consolation to those who love God, and all mankind for his sake; as well as *breaking down the partition-walls* which either the craft of the devil or the folly of men has built up; and of encouraging every child of God to say, (O when shall it once be!) "Whosoever doeth the will of my Father which is in heaven, the same is my brother, and sister, and mother." [34]

In this statement we find conjoined our concern for Christian unity, centered in our study of the Ephesian letter, and our Wesleyan

[31] "A Plain Account of the People Called Methodists."
[32] *Ibid.*
[33] *Ibid.*
[34] *Ibid.*, italics added.

heritage of openness and attention to a disciplined doing of the will of the Father.

Conclusion

We have noted that the relationship between Wesley's insistence upon an objective atonement wherein is justification and the subsequent discipline of life as instrumental to growth in obedience, Christlikeness, and pure love, is the very crux of his system of spiritual oversight. It is the nature of the Gospel, he said, "to save men not in sinning, but from sin." Cell has commented that

> when the Grace of God is seen only in the light of a transaction within the relation of God and Christ and not equally as a principle of holiness in the justified, such apprehension of the atonement has in the popular mind often fatally dulled the edge of conscience, dimmed the eye of the soul to the majesty of the moral law, weakened the moral will, covered the highest spark of divinity in man, namely, the moral recoil against all sin and unrighteousness, with the dead ashes of indifference.[35]

This pitfall Wesley strenuously avoided. In scripture and in experience he found the vocation to sinless perfection to be the corrective to the peril of faith without works, of religion without morality. Faith in the atonement was "the first principle of holiness and never a compensation for the lack of it." [36] The regimen of devotion, obedience, and service was insisted upon as instrumental to the restoration of the divine image and the fulfillment of perfect love. Wesley said: "God, whose judgment never can be contrary to the real nature of things, never can think me innocent or righteous or holy because another is so. He can no more, in this manner, confound me with Christ than with David or Abraham." [37] In these words Wesley commented on the Pauline statement: "He who through faith is righteous shall live." (Rom. 1:17 R.S.V.) The discipline of life through the means of grace is man's way of going forward in righteousness and true holiness. Wesley's insistence

[35] *Op. cit.,* p. 338.
[36] *Ibid.,* p. 342.
[37] Wesley, *Notes on the New Testament,* Romans I, 17.

upon both justification and sanctification has been said to be his original and unique synthesis of the Protestant ethic of grace with the Catholic ethic of holiness. The latter was purged of all merit and self-righteousness by Wesley's insistence that it was accomplished as the work of the Holy Spirit. In this Wesley was Arminian perhaps more even than he knew, for in his thought is seen the parallel of the famous trilogy of the Dutch "apostle of grace." In prevenient grace is the commencement of salvation; in enabling grace is the continuance of salvation; in sanctifying grace is the consummation of salvation.[38]

The recent renewal of interest in Reformation theology has reemphasized man's sinful plight and the necessity of justification by faith. Perhaps through our research in Wesleyan studies we can contribute to ecumenical Christianity an awareness of the responsibility which rests upon man for the discipline of life through the many and varied "means" of grace. We may profitably call attention to the necessity for sanctification by grace, manifesting itself in obedience, personal and social righteousness, and in holy love to God and fellow man, wrought in the life by the Holy Spirit.

[38] James Arminius, *Writings* (Grand Rapids: Baker Book House, 1956), I, p. 253.

10

The Unity of the Church

FREDERIC GREEVES

It is inevitable that discussion about Christian unity should begin with the fact of separated denominations. Unity thus tends to be considered from the point of view of division. We ask how unity may be "achieved" or "expressed," or how "reunion" may be made. Necessary as such an approach is for some purposes it is not the most fruitful, and it is not the one taken in this chapter. Rather we shall seek first to recall the centrality of the concept of unity in the Bible, and, secondly, the unique and distinctive character of Christian unity. The third section will deal with matters suggested by these earlier inquiries.

I

It is not too much to say that the whole of the Bible sounds the note of unity or one-ness. This is because both Testaments are monotheistic in their account of God and because both Testaments describe the mighty acts of God in calling and creating a people for his own possession. All thought about Christian unity must, therefore, be firmly grounded in the nature and the purpose of God himself. At the outset of our inquiry we must turn aside from all other concepts of unity or association, however useful some analogies may later prove to be. We can only know which analogies are serviceable when we know more about this unique unity.

1. Nothing about which the Bible speaks begins with statements about man; every declaration of scripture starts from a statement about God. So it is with unity. The first thing we have to learn is that God is ONE. Monotheism in the religion of Israel was more than a belief that God is the only God. Th. C. Vriezen has stressed that the Old Testament teaches both "God is *one* Being and God as *unique* Being." As he remarked, belief in the uniqueness of God existed whilst there was still belief that other gods existed; there was no God like Yahweh. But in the developed religion of the Hebrews, as notably in Deuteronomy, the uniqueness and the unity of God, though distinguishable, are closely related. As Vriezen put it, "The Unity indicates that God is not divided. His uniqueness means that Yahweh alone is God." [1]

It is the oneness of God that demands a total response from the whole man and from all his people. "Hear, O Israel, Yahweh our God, Yahweh is *one,* and you shall love the Lord your God with all your heart, and with all your soul and with all your might."

It is of supreme importance when we turn to the New Testament that we never lose sight of the fact that this passionate certainty that God is one dominated the minds of the first Christians. It was partly due to the unshakableness of this conviction that the Christology of the early Church developed as it did. Whatever Jesus meant, he could not mean any division or discord within the being of the one God. The doctrine of the Trinity is a doctrine about the unity of God, and it would be helpful if we could give wider currency to the term "Tri-unity."

[1] *An Outline of Old Testament Theology* (Newton Centre, Mass.: Charles T. Branford Company), p. 1751.

Contrary to opinions still widely expressed, the New Testament shows us very clearly that, in the words of one of the greatest living patristic scholars: "Christians were living *trinitarianly*" long before the time of councils and creeds. There is a host of passages in the New Testament in which Father, Son, and Spirit are associated together. They are associated always in the one Godhead, however, so that what is said of one may at other times be said of another and what is said of each is said of all.

It is, however, imperative to notice that Christian faith, from earliest days, was centered in a God who is both one and three. *A new concept of unity was born in this new understanding of God.* Social and family analogies used in exposition of the doctrine of the Trinity have been unpopular with most theologians, but we may be too afraid of such analogies. Certainly no other analogy is of much service. Because God is unique we cannot expect any comparison to be of much use, but at least we must say that when we think about God we must think of the supreme instance of "togetherness." This is part of what we mean when we say that God is love.

2. We shall return to this point shortly, but first we must notice the second truth on which the biblical emphasis upon unity is based. It has become almost a platitude now to say that the whole Bible is about God's covenant love and about the people of God. It is worth remembering, however, that only two or three generations ago few recognized this to be so. A young student in the nineteen-twenties noted and never forgot a lecturer's comment that the whole of the Bible was about two subjects—God and the Church. He noted it because it then seemed odd to speak of the Church in reference to the Old Testament and because it appeared to him to be obvious that while the New Testament has much to say about the Church its essential message is about the Kingdom.

Today we are all familiar with the recurrent themes that bind together books within the Testaments and the two Testaments with each other. Bible students talk about the concept of solidarity in Israel, about the prophetic insight into the universal purpose of God through the elect people, about the remnant, and about the

Son of man—a term with corporate as well as individual reference. We watch the people of God shrinking to the lonely Man on the cross, and we see New Israel being created as the Holy Spirit is given. We stand breathless at the fateful moment in the history of mankind before the gospel is taken to the Gentiles so that those who are not Abraham's kin may become Abraham's heirs. We recognize that the whole Bible is about the one people of God.

All this—and much more—is familiar to us, if not to the world. Do we, however, always recognize that the oneness of the people of God is dependent upon the oneness of God himself? And do we always recognize that this unity—this oneness—of the people of God is as essentially characteristic of that people as the divine oneness is of God himself?

That unity is of the *essence* of the Church is illustrated by most of the language used about the Church in the New Testament. It is, of course, impossible to gain more than a slight notion of New Testament doctrine about the Church if we limit ourselves to studying references to the word *ecclesia.* Even that word, however, is significant for our present purpose. Long ago F. J. A. Hort (*The Christian Ecclesia*) demonstrated that the references in the New Testament to "churches" in no way denies the primitive understanding of the oneness of the Church. For example, he wrote: "It is important to notice that not a word in Ephesians exhibits the one Ecclesia as made up of many Ecclesiae. . . . The members which make up the one Ecclesia are not communities but individual men."

It is, however, when we turn to other outstanding New Testament descriptions of the Church that its essential unity becomes more clear. These are "the people of God," "the Body of Christ," "the community [fellowship] of the Holy Spirit." In no instance could a plural noun be substituted; it is unthinkable that we should say "peoples," or "bodies," or "fellowships."

Paul S. Minear has made an exhaustive study of "*Images of the Church in the New Testament.*" Many of these images or analogies are of slighter importance and some of them occur infrequently. A study of them, however, shows very clearly that the vast majority have oneness or unity as a significant part of their meaning. To cite but a few, notice the following: "A letter from Christ; one loaf; the Bride of Christ, the vine or fig-tree, the flock, the Holy Temple, the holy nation. . . ." All this is no linguistic accident. It is only if we denigrate the word "Church" to mean a building, or a collection of individuals gathered for some specific purpose or on some particular occasion, that we can speak about "churches." There cannot be more than one Israel. God is one and so must be the people of God.

II

Having looked briefly at the central and fundamental importance of unity in the biblical revelation we turn to consider the *distinctive character* of unity in relation to the Church. In so doing we do not turn to other matters but look again at the truths already noticed.

1. The unity of the Church is a *participation in the unity of the triune God himself.*

While this is most plainly and movingly taught in John 17, it is also expressed in very many strands of the New Testament teaching—in far more than can be noticed here. If the Church be thought of as the company of those who are *en Christo,* then it must be remembered that this "in" is a unique use of that preposition. All spatial reference is lost; it can also be said that Christ is *in us.* We are "one in him" because we all profess a common Lord and because we share in the one baptism; we have all been buried with Christ and are risen with him; we live in him and he in us. It is "in him" that we meet; in him we *inevitably* meet.

If it is as the *koinonia* that we consider the Church, then our fellowship with each other is not merely a way in which we demonstrate or seek to deepen our participation in the Spirit; it is the very meaning of that participation. It is impossible to receive the Spirit without being brought together with others who receive him.

All this is made plain—or as plain as it can be to human eyes in this world—in the high priestly prayer of Jesus (John 17). Here, as C. H. Dodd and others have pointed out, we are given a picture of a "triangular relationship" between the Father and the Son, the Son and the disciples, and the disciples with one another.

The unity that we are to enjoy is not only to be *comparable* with the unity between Father and Son—though that is wonderful enough. It is to be part of the same unity. "As thou, Father, art in me, and I in thee, so also may they be *in us.*" In that one sentence is summed up the deepest meaning of Christian unity. Of John 17, William Temple—than whom no man has better served the cause of Christian unity nor displayed a greater gift for bringing Christians to a common mind—wrote:

> Before the loftiness of that hope and calling our little experience of unity and fellowship is humbled to the dust. Our friendships, our reconciliations, our unity of spirit in Church gatherings or in missionary conferences—beautiful as these are, and sometimes even wonderful in comparison with our habitual life of sectional rivalries and tensions, yet how poor and petty they are in the light of the Lord's longing.

We should not, however, be content to speak about "our Lord's longing," as though this were a *totally* unanswered prayer. In Temple's own thought there was a strange dichotomy, so that he could say—quite inconsistently with much of his own finest teaching—"I believe in the Holy Catholic Church and sincerely regret that it does not at present exist." Rather, we must agree with what Temple himself said at the opening service of the Edinburgh Conference, 1937:

> The unity of the Church, on which our faith and hope rest, is grounded in the unity of God and the uniqueness of His redeeming act in Jesus Christ. The "one body and the one spirit" correspond to the "one God and Father of all." The unity of the Church of God is a perpetual fact; our task is not to create it but to exhibit it.[2]

[2] For comment and quotations from Temple see P. Hartill, *The Unity of God* (London: Mowbray & Company, Ltd., 1952), pp. 149 ff.

In so far as we have our access to the one Father in the one Lord through the one Spirit, we are thereby brought into relation with all who share that privilege. However far away from them we feel ourselves to be, however far from us they think they are, we cannot in reality escape from each other. To be redeemed is to be brought into the redeemed family; to be in Christ is to be members of the one Body, to receive the Holy Spirit is to be made sharers in the *koinonia* of the Spirit.

Even if we are together in enmity, we are together. That is why there is something peculiarly sinful about divisions in Christendom. As civil war is more horrible than conflict between nations and family hatreds are more diabolical than strife between strangers, so—but more—disunity among Christians is grievous, shameful, and destructive.

It is this truth which is, at long last, beginning to disturb and to humble many Christians in many denominations. We have for some time sought to find a way of coming together; we are now beginning to find that we *are together* precisely because we are Christians at all. Now we see the true shame and scandal of our divisions. They are no longer to be thought of as divisions between rival parties or separated associations; they are divisions in God's one family, and that is why no other word for them is possible than "sinful."

2. If unity is thus part of the very meaning of Christian life itself, and therefore one of the primary meanings of the Church's existence, it is also part of the meaning of the Church's *mission*.

In the first section of this chapter we saw that the biblical story is about the oneness of God and the oneness of his purpose to create one people; now we notice that Christian unity is *in itself* the purpose for which the Church is created.

God creates the Church for himself—in order that he may possess a people of his own who glorify him. But God's love is extended to all mankind and the method of his love is reconciliation. It is quite insufficient, though it is necessary, to think of the Church as commissioned by God to *offer* his reconciling love to all men.

The Church is to be the evidence of the truth of the gospel; it is to be the gospel manifested. The Church is itself that to which the gospel invites all men.

If anything is clear in the New Testament it is surely that the love of the brethren for each other in the one Body, the *koinonia* of those who share in the Spirit, the oneness of the people of God, is to be *the* evangelical witness and power. This is so plain that it is almost unbelievable that we Christians could ever forget it. The fact that we would perhaps find it difficult to say that the one supreme need for every human being is to "come to Church" shows how the word "Church" has been stripped of most of its meaning. The fact that we should be embarrassed if we found ourselves saying, "If you want to know what the gospel is, and to be sure that it is true, look at us and come with us," shows how far we are from the basic facts of New Testament religion.

Above all, the fact that we think of unity as something that we need to "achieve" for this or that good, practical reason, shows how far we have wandered from the real meaning of Christian unity. There is one God and there is one Church; these two facts are inseparable. That "all may be one" can never be for Christians a slogan comparable to other ambitions. The unity of which we now speak is grounded in God himself and in his revealed purpose for mankind. It is in oneness alone that the Church can exist; it is in oneness alone that the Church can witness; it is to that oneness that God invites all mankind. All the really difficult problems in the way of what we call "Christian unity" are problems about *division*. Without stretching the analogy too far, we may say that just as the difficulties that faced those who formulated Trinitarian dogma was to describe the "Three" within the "One," so the difficulty that faces Christendom today is to see how the many can be reconciled with the one. The only use of that similitude is to remind us that with the Church, as with God himself, the basic fact is unity. If we start from there we may begin to see both our present divergences and our future way more clearly.

III

In the closing section of this chapter a few implications that follow from what has been said call for mention. If most of these are negative in character they may at least serve to clear the ground for constructive thinking.

1. In the first place a number of *alternatives* to full organic unity are found to be unsatisfactory.

A. Firstly we must reject two attempts which are made to account for disunity by denying its existence. On the one hand, there is the view—characteristic of Rome—that the one Church exists in the Roman communion and that all other Christians—"the separated brethren"—have fallen away. I do not propose to discuss that view. On the other hand, there are those who deny that there is any significant division because "all Christians are one in spirit."

This concept of "spiritual" as distinct from visible and "organizational" unity is a most misleading and disastrous one. It is misleading because it uses the term "spiritual" in a totally nontheological sense. It implies that some characteristic of human beings—for example, their shared ideas, their particular interpretation of religious experience, or even their faith—is the all-important matter. We should be wise never to use the term "spiritual" save in reference to the Holy Spirit and his work. It is because there is one Spirit that there is one Body; it is not through any merit or quality of our own—not even our faith—that we are made one; it is through him alone. This notion of "spiritual unity" is disastrous because it leads to complacency about our divisions.

The term "organic" (used about unity) is often a cause of perplexity. It is as an analogy that belongs to the "Body" concept of the Church. Its whole point is that the members of the one body cannot be separated; a dismembered limb or bodily organ is dead. If we were in fact separated from the whole Body of Christ we should not be Christians at all. This is part of what Methodists mean when they say—as British Methodists do in their official statement: "The Methodist Church claims and cherishes its place in the Holy Catholic Church, which is the Body of Christ." It is the very nature of the Church on earth to be visible; it is, therefore, characteristic of unity that it should be visible. If we think of the Church as the people or family of God it follows that unity must be, not only a vague so-called "spiritual" association but a full, active, and manifest family life.

At this point we are reminded of a slogan often used in defense of Christian divisions: "Unity but not uniformity." Of course the members of a body differ, otherwise there would be no body; of course the members of a family are different from each other elsewise there would not be a family. Of course within the one Church there will be variety of many kinds. But a family that cannot eat together, that cannot manifest love for each other in concrete actions, and that takes the greatest pains to see that its members do not meet on the more important occasions of their common life is no family.

We may indeed hazard the guess that it is only in a united family that rich variety among the members can fully exist. In our different denominations we are so afraid of losing what we like to call "our special emphases," and we are so on guard lest we should be guilty of looking too like some of our Christian brethren, that the life of each denomination is restricted and impoverished. The Roman is almost afraid of his own doctrine of justification by grace alone lest he should be guilty of Protestantism; the Methodist is held back from liturgical richness and from discovering, for example, the meaning of confession and absolution for fear that he might be mistaken for a "Catholic" or an "Anglican." In the fully realized life of the people of God, in unimpeded organic existence in the body of Christ, we should begin to discover the endless variety of unity.

B. The second kind of false alternative to true unity that must be mentioned is the attempt to base unity upon some one or other limited foundation.

There is, for example, the notion of *confessional churches.* Whether in the more sectarian form, as in the splinter groups of

Plymouth Brethren, or in the concept of Pan-Methodism, Pan-Lutheranism, et cetera, this is an ideal which must be rejected as totally inadequate. That there should be close association between Christians of like mind is desirable, though a firm limit should be put to such association. We must never, however, confuse the togetherness of those who are associated because they have similar historical origins and share similar convictions and religious experiences with the oneness of the people of God. In fact, the larger such a group becomes the more easy it is for its members to ignore other Christians.

On the other hand, we must also reject the notion of *national churches* as an alternative to the full unity of Christendom. That all Christians in one place should be recognized as members of the one Christ is indeed highly necessary, but there is all the difference between speaking of the Church *in* England, Africa, or Germany and in speaking of the Church *of* any particular country. Christians belong to a heavenly kingdom; accidents of birth or dwelling place are no more revelant to the unity in Christ than are peculiarities of temperament. Our citizenship is in heaven, and we should not behave here as though there were separate "heavens" for denominations or nations.

For similar reasons we must reject the idea of *federation* as a substitute for organic unity. That separated denominations should work together is obviously much better than that they should work in opposition or indifference to each other. Even secular organizations work together; such co-operation reflects no credit upon those who are made one in Christ and gives no glory to the Lord. The most powerful argument in favor of federal churches was made by P. T. Forsyth in *The Church and the Sacraments.* I have recently reread his arguments. They do not seem to me to be substantiated even by his own premises, and it is impossible to doubt that had that prophetic thinker, so far ahead of his times, lived to encounter both modern biblical scholarship and the ecumenical movement he would have reversed his judgment.

Indeed, one of Forsyth's own illustrations shows us the limitations in the federal idea. Pointing out that many visitors to Cambridge, having seen the colleges, ask to be shown "the University," he said, "You cannot show the University—which yet is Cambridge. Who can deny the University?" This he applied to the denominations. The Church is not a University, however. Actual—to some degree—as may be the oneness of the University of Cambridge, the oneness of the Church is a very different matter. It is proper that a student should be asked which college he wishes to enter, but we should never lose our sense of shame that a convert to Christianity has to ask, "Which church should I join?" Both the suggestion of alternatives and the impression that one "joins" a church as one enters a college or joins a club are the bitter result of the sin of the Church.

2. Such are some of the negative conclusions to which our inquiry has led. A few positive ones must be very briefly suggested.

A. The greatest of all errors about Christian unity is to imagine that we can see *in advance* what the one Church would be like in its complete manifestation. To believe in the triune God it is not necessary to know precisely what he is like. We begin to know him better and to know more about him as *we live in him.* It is only in the one Church that men and women will discover more fully what the one Church is. Only a united Church can hope for an adequate theology. This is the venture of faith to which God calls us—to go out not knowing whither we go, but to go out together with him.

B. Secondly, important as it is to be sure what is necessary for the Church to "be the Church"—and with that subject this chapter does not deal—it is no less urgent to recognize that the Church militant is the Church of pardoned *sinners.* Visser t'Hooft in a too little known book, *The Renewal of the Church,* pointed out that it is only when the Church is aware of its perpetual need for renewal and knows how that renewal may be found that it is able to hold together the two apparently opposite convictions that the Church must be *one* and that it must be *holy.* Though we should hesitate to admit the fact, we are often so afraid of being contaminated by some of our fellow Christians that we hold back from them. There is no reason to expect that the one Church, in its earthly part, would be free from sin; there is every reason to hope that together we should grow in sanctity. The notion that first each denomination must become purified and then we may come together is to be rejected.

C. In conclusion it must be noted that unity is primarily a matter for each local "church" and, indeed, for each individual Christian. Necessarily our minds are now much occupied with the healing of denominational divisions, but it will be as each denomination and each "society" within it grows in the unity about which we have been thinking that each will make a contribution toward the wider unity. Our Methodist emphasis upon fellowship could enable us to make this fact very plain.

If unity is to be found in the small or large group it must exist in the heart of each individual. This is part of the uniqueness of Christian unity that it is a most personal, even private matter. We find unity only in Christ through the Holy Spirit and, though God's purpose is for all mankind, the entrance gate is personal faith. Of each as well as of all it is true—to quote William Temple again—that "The true quality of unity is the consequence of the *doxa,* the glory, which is the quality of life of the new creation in Christ." "When anyone is united to Christ, there is a new world" (II Cor. 5:17 N.E.B.). "You are all one person in Christ Jesus" (Gal. 3:28 N.E.B.).

We must pray and work that we may "attain the unity inherent in our faith and our knowledge of the Son of God" (Eph. 4:13).

11

The Church and Modern Man

F. THOMAS TROTTER

It is very proper that this institute be devoted to the study of the nature of the Church. In that direction we have necessarily delved into the questions of history and doctrine and sought to find those marks of the people of God which ought to be our *raison d'etre.*

Implicit in all our discussion have been the persistent, if not always stated, questions: What is the nature of the self-understanding of the modern world? How does the man of the mid-century locate himself in relation to the Church? In what ways does the Church need to frame its witness to God in Christ in order to speak to man's condition? Such questions have been behind most of our papers and all our conversations. Of course, any theologizing today, done without reference to the apologetic imperative, is likely to be mere dilletantism.

The observation that we live in a *new* time with immense new problems is commonplace. This period has been described as the "post-Christian era," as "the time of the world come of age," or, in Romano Guardini's phrase, the "end of the modern world." Modern man, if indeed he may still be called "modern," has become what he is within a few generations. The swiftness of this change in man's self-understanding has left the Church puzzled in its apologetic. The Church often is discovered to be answering questions that have not been asked. While it persists in the undoubtedly important work of mining Christian history and traditions, those very traditions are being called into radical doubt. Classically defined as in "God's image," man finds more understandable an art show entitled the "new images of man"—which displayed a poignantly macabre exhibition of dessicated, emaciated, and haunted forms. This is a form of what Paul Tillich likes to call the "questions" being asked of the Church. I once heard a churchman say to Tillich, in reference to such art, "What are we going to do about this *ugly* art?" Tillich winced visibly and then replied, "Please, say it is *impoverished,* but don't say it is ugly." Such a question points the Christian conscience to witness, not to judgment. In the light of classical Christian values—or what we may have assumed were values—and in the light of the changing, sometimes violent, new images of man, the Church is called radically to examine its preaching and its life. Ortega y Gasset wrote: "I am compelled to conclude that even the most gifted among us . . . have not the slightest suspicion that the pointer in the compass of western sensibility is veering through at least ninety degrees." [1]

I propose, therefore, in this chapter, to do three things: First, I will attempt to describe in admittedly general terms the image of the Church in the modern world, noting something of its style and touching on some of the characterizations of the Church in recent literature; second, I will suggest two types of "religious" responses to the Church in the light of the issues of the mid-century, the movements of "out-flanking" and "attack"; finally, and briefly, I will indicate some of the suggestions advanced by Christian thinkers to cope with the issues of the modern world.

[1] *The Modern Theme,* translated by James Cleugh (New York: Harper & Row, Publishers, 1961), p. 20.

The Image of the Church in the "Age of the Apocalypse"

When we look at our times we cannot but notice the symptom which Emmanuel Mounier has called "the apocalyptic consciousness." This mood fairly permeates Western culture. One has only to turn to the arts—sensitive barometers to man's spiritual condition—to find evidence of the extent of this mood: "Waiting" (Beckett); "the age of vigil" (Scott); "the age of longing" (Koestler); "the seventh seal" (Bergman).

There is abroad a widespread feeling that some cataclysmic event is at hand. Modern man lives under the seemingly permanent threat of nuclear annihilation. He has approached what Jaspers calls "the borders of possibility" beyond which lies catastrophe.

The images which dominate the writings of the most sensitive commentators of our time are often borrowed from Christian apocalypticism. Samuel Beckett uses specific allusions in his *Waiting for Godot;* Ignazio Silone does also in his *Bread and Wine.* Important films, such as Fellini's *La Dolce Vita* and Bergman's *The Seventh Seal,* are modern paraphrases of the revelation of John. While the artist is attracted to the apocalyptic imagery in the biblical materials, however, he makes significant revision. Ironically, the most essential Christian element, the eschatological dimension of hope, is missing. The modest achievement of Beckett's heroes, for example, is simply that "they have kept their appointment." The text for Bergman's apocalypse is Rev. 8:1: "When the Lamb opened the seventh seal, there was silence in heaven about half an hour." Ominous image—the measurable pause before the end!

The late Robinson Jeffers viewed the decline of Christian culture and the rise of modern culture as the prelude to man's doom:

Look, there are two curves in the air: the air
That man's fate breathes: there is the rise and fall
  of the Christian culture-complex, that broke
  its dawn cloud
Fifteen centuries ago, and now past noon
Drifts to decline; and there's the yet vaster curve, but

mostly in the future, of the age that began at
Kittyhawk
Within one's lifetime.—The first of these curves passing
its noon and the second orient
All in one's little lifetime make it seem pivotal.
Truly the time is marked by insane splendors and agonies.
But watch when the two curves cross: you children
Not far way down the hawk's-nightmare future: you will
see monsters.[2]

We live in a time of "insane splendors and agonies" and wonder at what monsters lie in wait down the "hawk's-nightmare future." Or, to borrow W. B. Yeats's compelling lines:

And what rough beast, its hour come round at last,
Slouches toward Bethlehem to be born? [3]

Three Characteristics of Modern Man

There is widespread agreement that modern man—we members of the human race who happen to be living in the mid-century—is undergoing severe shifts in his self-understanding. He is a problem to himself, to his neighbors, and, I am sure, even to God. He is certainly a problem to me; because I am not quite sure how I proceed with any confidence at all to describe this mythical person. Therefore I have chosen simply to describe what it occurs to me is a fairly accurate picture of the cross section of American man and American religion. I am sure that there will be significant modifications from country to country.

1. *My mythical man is a biblical illiterate.*

The enormous publishing successes of the Revised Standard and the New English Bibles notwithstanding, most of our contemporaries own Bibles but few read them. As has been pointed out by Strawson, the loss of biblical language and imagery creates an im-

[2] "Diagram." Copyright 1948 by Robinson Jeffers. Reprinted from *The Double Axe and Other Poems* by Robinson Jeffers by permission of Random House, Inc.

[3] "The Second Coming." Used by permission of The Macmillan Company, New York; Macmillan and Company of Canada, Ltd.; Mrs. W. B. Yeats; and A. P. Watt & Son.

poverishment in sacrament and in hymn singing. A whole category of humor has arisen around the theme of the confusion and ignorance about the Bible.

This represents a most serious fact in defining our modern man. He stands—particularly in America—deaf to the gospel unless it is demythologized into the colloquial. An example of his helplessness may be seen in this whole matter of "apocalyptic consciousness."

Many Christians find this literary world of apocalyptic images a strange one indeed. This is due in part to the widespread disinterest in biblical apocalypticism in the liberal phase of American religion, but more generally to the debiblicized nature of modern church practice. The average Christian in the U.S.A. normally is almost incapable of understanding imaginative biblical literature. The source of his religious faith is not necessarily the Bible or tradition, but a vague sort of self-validating notion of "experience." Kathleen Bliss noted that "theologians today are being asked to write for an audience which scarcely knows its Bible, and uses, in the ordinary traffic of life, a language farther removed from biblical concepts than any has been for ages." [4]

An example drawn from Shakespearean criticism may illustrate this point. In recent years, critics like G. Wilson Knight of Leeds and Roy Battenhouse of Indiana have indicated a substantial case for a criticism of Shakespeare based upon Christian myth. General reluctance to accept this hypothesis is based upon the inability of the modern critic seriously to consider the possibility that there was a time when men generally and naturally thought in Christian categories. In a recent study of this problem J. A. Bryant wrote:

> The average Elizabethan . . . would probably have sat, or stood, through a Shakespeare play without noticing the astonishing number of allusions to Scripture, Prayer Book, and dogma generally. He would have missed them because to him they were commonplace; we miss them because to us they are almost completely foreign, and their strangeness seems but a part of the general strangeness of an unfamiliar language.[5]

[4] Evanston Report, *Christian Century* (1954).
[5] *Hippolyta's View* (Lexington: University of Kentucky Press, 1961), p. 15.

2. *My mythical modern man's religion is essentially sentimentalism.*

Religious sentimentalism, or "religiosity" as Vahanian has called it, is a deeply seated trend in modern American religion. It takes a variety of forms, but most generally it is characterized by an accent on emotional validation and a suspicion of the dogmatic or traditional. Particularly prevalent expressions of this syndrome include the blasphemous "names" for God such as "the man upstairs," "my friend," "the ever-loving doll," or simply "He." Recently in America a popular song was widely admired, the lyrics of which were "Faith, hope, and charity, That's how to live successfully." The mass popularity of Werner Sallman's "Head of Christ" measures this sentimentalism. John Dixon, a prominent Methodist art critic, has described this portrait as one of an "un-sexed matinee idol dressed in a department store nightgown." A further expression of this mood in American life has been the phenomenon called "piety on the Potomac." The surest way to rile tempers in politics today is to suggest that sentimental religious slogans and other pious gymnastics have no place in either politics *or* religion.

The sources of religiosity are deep in recent Western history. As has been suggested earlier in this volume, the emphasis of Wesley on "inward religion" became, in the nineteenth century, an emphasis on "the religion of inwardness." As Karl Barth and Paul Tillich have both carefully suggested in relation to the problem of Schleiermacher's famous definition of religion, the nineteenth century generally chose to accent the subjective rather than the objective side of his formula. The transcendent otherness of God was swallowed up in pious feelings about God. One of the ironies of the current evangelistic efforts of Billy Graham, vast though the operation may be, is the fact that his message is, by and large, proclaimed in the language of the recent past. Nostalgia is the prime ingredient in religiosity. This spills over into a whole nexus of outworn ideologies, including moral, social, and political views, so that in contemporary American life the specter of an extremist right in politics has openly challenged the easy accommodations of the

Church's gospel to the world. This is done in the name of religion and seems only further to convince the cultured despisers on the left that the Church is outmoded in the twentieth century.

3. *My mythical modern man is a specialist, a technician, and he sees religion as having but limited relevance and hegemony in life.*

One of the fruits of overspecialization in the modern world is the gradual withering away of the Church's authority in the world. This trend, more like a mass movement in the last generation, has produced both universal acceptance of an infinite clamor of truth claims, on the one hand, and strangely myopic vision on the other. Ortega has called the modern man *Naturmensch*—he has contempt for tradition and principles and he adopts a "primitive" attitude toward anything outside his "field." Specialization continues. Universities find increasingly and mutually exclusive departments neither speaking to nor understanding each other.

While specialization brings primitive attitudes in most areas, it also brings men the kind of assurance that comes from authority and knowledge in a specialization and the abdication of responsibility and knowledgeability in other sectors. With notable exceptions, scientists producing the fearful nuclear weapons of our time assume that moral dilemmas involved are the problems of theologians and politicians. Karl Jaspers, in his notable study, *Man in the Modern Age,* wrote:

> In the false clarity which is created by the consciousness of technique and of man's life as the consciousness of the production of all things, the true inwardness of the indubitably unconditioned is lost. Religion as the historical basis of human existence has become, so to say, invisible. . . . Religious faith actively held by individuals grows continually rarer.[6]

The World's View of the Church

Amos Wilder's suggestion in his important little book *Theology and Modern Literature* is that the modern writer often attacks the

[6] Garden City, N. Y.: Doubleday & Company, Inc., 1933, p. 152. Used by permission of Routledge & Kegan Paul, Ltd.

desiccated character of the Church's religiosity from the point of view of the prophetic insights of gospel itself. The term "vestigial moralities" does not imply ethics alone, but that region of a society's life where morals, values, manners, and, above all, taste overlap. Wilder wrote:

> The greatest handicaps to creative social behavior are rigidity and obtuseness. In religious groups these are often encouraged by moral dogma and habit. In this area, the agnostic today, as over against the church, is not only emancipated and indifferent; he is caustic, if not vituperative.[7]

Rigidity and obtuseness encouraged by moral dogma and habit—a description that is more often accurate than we like to feel. This provides a fertile field for an attack upon the Church in modern literature, ranging all the way from the debunking and serio-comic to the sophisticated and literate. This tendency is so general as to be an almost permanent formula in modern literature. As such it represents an immense barrier to effective communication of the gospel, on the one hand, and acceptance within the church of the prophetic warnings of modern literature, on the other.

The "debunking" school of literary attack on the Church is the most obvious and least effective criticism. The most famous practitioner of this form of criticism was probably Sinclair Lewis. His scathing attack upon the Church was unrelieved. One has only to read *Elmer Gantry* to be reminded that debunking, indeed, was Lewis' forte. Describing his hero, Lewis wrote that Gantry "never said anything important, and he always said it sonorously. He could make 'good morning' seem profound as Kant, welcoming as a brass band, and uplifting as a cathedral organ." Lewis' attack was precise and measured to prick the conscience of any who seriously pondered the problem of the communication of the gospel. Describing Gantry's Sunday school background, Lewis noted that Gantry "had, in fact, got everything from church and Sunday school except, perhaps, any longing whatever for decency and kind-

[7] Cambridge, Mass.: Harvard University Press, 1958, p. 113.

ness and reason." In one respect this is a *prophetic* protest against the vestigial morality and religiosity of the American culture religion. To that extent it is honest and hard hitting. On the other hand, Lewis was unmerciful in his protest. There is no hope, no grace. One has only to compare the novel itself with Richard Brooks's exciting adaptation of it in the film. Brooks added sympathy to the negative witness of Lewis and made it a much more powerful human story, but the symbol of "Gantryism" is forever with us.

An obscure, but typical, debunker of the same period was Herbert Asbury, a distant relative of Bishop Asbury, one of the founding fathers of The Methodist Church. Asbury wrote a lighthearted but devastating book entitled *Up from Methodism.* He had become so embittered with the vestigial morality of his Southern Methodist background that he produced this book which now seems a bit intemperate. We must remember, however, that it was written in the decade of the Darrow-Bryan debates on evolution, the temperance movement, H. L. Mencken, and Elmer Gantry. Typical of Asbury's style is this passage:

> [The Preacher] made it quite clear, out of his profound knowledge of the wishes of the Almighty, that God did not want little boys and girls to have a good time. Quite the contrary. God wanted them to do exactly what the Preacher told them to do; He wanted them to accept the Preacher as their guide and their philosopher and to believe everything they were told, without fretting him with unanswerable and therefore blasphemous questions. He wanted the little boys and girls to spend most of their time praying to Him to "gimme this and gimme that," and the rest of it being little gentlemen and little ladies, solemn and subdued, speaking only when spoken to and answering promptly when called. God told the Preacher, who relayed the message on to me very impressively, that it was a sin to play marbles on Sunday, or to play for keeps at any time; that it was a sin to roll hoops on the sidewalk in front of the church or rattle a stick against the picket fence in front of the parsonage. Everything that I wanted to do, everything that seemed to hold any promise of fun or excitement, was a sin.[8]

[8] New York: Alfred A. Knopf, Inc., 1926, pp. 69-70.

William Faulkner explored exhaustively the theme of the vestigial morality. One might even venture the suggestion that the fall of the Compson family and the rise of the Snopes family, the collapse of the old order and its moralities and the rise of a new order and its amoralities, represents an imaginative statement of the moral ambiguities of our time. Quentin in *The Sound and the Fury* is a good example of this problem. Wilder wrote:

> We see the meager and irremediably injured early years of the children, the prenatal history, as it were, of later giant traumas and obsessions; the inculcation of social and racial distortions; the inbreeding of desiccated, feudal-Christian survivals in the son Quentin.[9]

The Sound and the Fury is set in the framework of Easter week, 1928. Faulkner, apparently, set his novel directly in the middle of the central theme of Christian faith, the resurrection. Easter for the Compson family is measured simply by the fact that the Negro servants have been allowed to attend church that day and, therefore, the Sunday dinner will be modest and cold. Easter equals "cold cuts" for the Compsons.

In Faulkner's Snopes family trilogy we see his view that the desiccated morality of "religious" people is so conditioned by selfish and pre-Christian motivation that any transcendence is problematic. Indeed the gospel itself becomes the basis for a new tyranny.

> . . . ours [is] a town established and decreed by people neither Catholics nor Protestants nor even atheists but incorrigible nonconformists, nonconformists not just to everybody else but to each other in mutual accord; a nonconformism defended and preserved by descendants whose ancestors hadn't quitted home and security for a wilderness in which to find freedom of thought as they claimed and oh yes, believed, but to find freedom in which to be incorrigible and unreconstructible Baptists and Methodists; not to escape from tyranny as they claimed and believed, but to establish one.[10]

[9] *Op. cit.*, p. 120.
[10] *The Town* (New York: Random House, 1957), p. 307.

A button-down collar expression of the same theme is to be found in J. D. Salinger's writings. Recent studies indicate that Salinger is very likely the most popular single writer with American college students today, if not with certain high-school parent groups. His *Catcher in the Rye* has enjoyed phenomenal success since publication. Holden Caulfield, confused and neurotic though he is, is able to point accurately at the soft spots in conventional piety and vestigial religion in our time.

Salinger is at his critical best in *Franny and Zooey* when he has Zooey express himself on the "flabbiness" of much modern religion. He takes the form of criticizing the sentimental amalgam of Jesus and Buddha and Saint Francis. Franny represents the type of confused modern religiosity which is uneasy in the atmosphere of vestigial morality and reacts by being emancipated; e.g., reading Buddhism and other exotic literature, on the one hand, but, on the other, being desperately confused about the earthy and commonplace arena of grace—namely, the place where men live and work and play. In a striking passage, Zooey tells Franny that her search for religious authenticity is sentimental.

Another approach found in the criticism of religion in modern literature is the expression of the apparent loss of confidence in traditional religious practices in themselves. Graham Greene's characters while nominally and even active Roman Catholics, often express the *ennui* and disinterestedness of a nonbeliever. Querry, for example, when asked by Rycker what he prays for when he prays, replies, "I ask for a teddy bear." Albert Camus' characters work out their salvation totally outside the context of the Church. T. S. Eliot, often thought of as the spokesman for a Christian criticism in modern literature, shares this judgment that the rites of faith now seem problematic. Celia, in *The Cocktail Party,* is embarrassed to discuss theological matters because for her family religion simply did not exist:

> Well, my bringing up was pretty conventional—
> I had always been taught to disbelieve in sin.

Oh, I don't mean that it was ever mentioned!
But anything wrong, from our point of view
Was either bad form, or was psychological.[11]

Possibly the most consistent attack in modern literature upon the formal and moribund character of religion is to be found in the writings of Franz Kafka, in particular in his short story entitled "At Our Synagogue" and in such allusions as the famous Cathedral scene in *The Trial.* Joseph K., a bank clerk, has been asked to show a visitor the city's cathedral. He wonders why he was chosen for the task. Then he recalls that sometime earlier, although he is no longer associated with the movement, he had been an active member in The Society for the Preservation of Ancient Monuments.

One of the most sophisticated of these expressions of disenchantment with Christian institutions is to be found in Wallace Stevens' poem "Sunday Morning." He pictures a woman sitting on the veranda of her home on Sunday morning, dreamingly recalling religious images of ages of faith.

Complacencies of the peignoir, and the late
Coffee and oranges in a sunny chair,
And the green freedom of a cockatoo
Upon a rug, mingle to dissipate
The holy hush of ancient sacrifice.
She dreams a little, and she feels the dark
Encroachment of that old catastrophe,
As a calm darkens among water-lights.
The pungent oranges and bright green wings
Seem things in some procession of the dead,
Winding across wide water, without sound.
The day is like wide water, without sound,
Stilled for the passing of her dreaming feet
Over the seas, to silent Palestine,
Dominion of the blood and sepulcher.[12]

[11] Used by permission of Harcourt, Brace & World, Inc., and Faber and Faber, Ltd.

[12] From *Collected Poems of Wallace Stevens* (New York: Alfred A. Knopf, Inc.). Used by permission of the publisher.

The dressing gown, the late coffee and pungent oranges, and the dissipation of the holy hush of ancient sacrifice—these things symbolize the loss of roots in the Christian tradition for many of the most sensitive men and women in our time.

Two Possible Responses

Modern man has assumed two stances with regard to the classical Christian tradition. He has, on the one hand, simply "outflanked" that tradition and created what amounts to a new and secular faith. On the other hand, he has "attacked" the tradition and sought to reconstruct meaningful human existence on the ruins of classical Christianity.

Outflanking God

Franklin Baumer, in his provocative book *Religion and the Rise of Scepticism,* locates the origins of the modern secular faith in the work of the Enlightenment. Because of the obvious penalties imposed on theologians who dared to suggest radical revisions of the orthodox dogma, the sensitive and imaginative thinkers developed the convenient device of "outflanking" and, thereby, relegating Christian categories to irrelevancy. Kant's achievement, "religion within the bounds of pure reason," is generally a perfect expression of the program of the development of rationalism "around" Christianity. This was to lead to the development of the triumph of science in the nineteenth century. Baumer notes that the *Summa Theologica* was to the thirteenth century as the *Encyclopedia of the Arts, Sciences, and Crafts* was to the eighteenth century. The tendency of the rationalistic movement in religion in the seventeenth century and onward was to make "religion" (the first commandment) supplemental to "ethics" (the second commandment).[13]

Inevitably a "utopian" spirit begins to dominate the rationalistic thrust. Rational society, for Condorcet is to be

an asylum in which the memory of his persecutors does not follow him, an asylum in which, living in imagination with mankind re-established in

[13] Cf. Baumer (New York: Harcourt, Brace & World, Inc., 1960), p. 59.

its rights and in its true nature, he can forget mankind corrupted and tormented by greed, fear, envy. It is in this asylum that he truly lives with his fellows, in a *heaven* which his reason has created, and which his love of humanity embellishes with the purest joys.[14]

One cannot overlook the enormous strides made by civilization during this period of rational and scientific progress. In the perspective of time, however, we see how much it cost man in human terms. I need not dwell on the widely documented phenomena of the development of this movement. Let it suffice to indicate that the culmination of this movement has not been a free man but a slave man. As Tillich, Guardini, Jaspers, and others are pointing out, the utopian tradition has tended to create a man who is not autonomous, but dominated by technology and rational abstraction. This has led to the successive shocks of the twentieth century which have badly jolted modern man out of his complacency regarding his own ability to cope with existence. Jaspers has the most incisive description of the feeling of "terrible impotence" that has been the legacy of rationalism in our time. With the loss of transcendence, man's hopes are anchored in the possibility of earthly fulfillment and perfection. But since his finitude requires that his powers of intervention and control are ultimately limited, he cannot hope to control events decisively. Jaspers wrote:

One inspired with a religious conviction that man was naught in the face of Transcendence was unperturbed by changing events. Changes were the outcome of God's will, and were not felt to clash with other conceivable possibilities. Today, however, the price which aims at universal understanding, and the arrogance of one who regards himself as master of the world and therefore wants to mould it to his liking, knock at all doors, while their frustration arouses a feeling of terrible impotence.[15]

Destroying God

A later reaction to the utopian mood of secular religious faith is "nihilism," the peculiar form of faith which seeks to attack Chris-

[14] *Heavenly City of the Eighteenth-Century Philosophers,* translated by Carl Becker, pp. 150-51. Quoted in Baumer, *ibid.,* p. 75.

[15] *Op. cit.,* p. 3.

tianity rather than outflank it. As Kant's dictum, "religion within the bounds of pure reason" may serve as the description of the former movement, the French revolutional slogan, "erase the infamy," will serve to describe the attack.

The growing dominance of this type of religious thinking in the twentieth century is directly related to the collapse of the values and hopes of the 19th century. Heine is the first modern voice in this form of thinking, but it is the enigmatic German Nietzsche to whom we turn for the fullest expression of the mood. For Nietzsche God is dead. Nietzsche had the kind of honesty that hit hard at the very center of faith itself. For Nietzsche the skeptical tradition had moved into a new phase which was both qualitatively and quantitatively different from previous phases. In this phase the intellectual classes did not seek merely to convict the Christian God with weapons of reason, but, as Baumer noted, "They drew their knives and assassinated God himself." [16] It is no coincidence that writers of our generation have turned to Nietzsche as the author and prophet of the hard times in which we find ourselves. In the beautiful passage in *The Joyful Wisdom* Nietzsche wrote:

> We ourselves, readers of riddles, born soothsayers, who wait as it were on the mountain-tops, somewhere between yesterday and tomorrow and contradictorily harnessed between the two, we the premature firstborn of the century to come, who should already have perceived the shadows that will envelop Europe, why do we await the rise of this black tide without any real interest, even without fear or anxiety for ourselves.[17]

God died for Nietzsche, not primarily because the concept was useless, but that what man called God was not worthy of God. In a pregnant passage in *Thus Spake Zarathustra* Nietzsche expressed his anger and frustration with the intellectual and religious posture of the nineteenth century: "I have moved out of the house of the learned and slammed the door behind me. For too long my

[16] *Op. cit.*, p. 129.
[17] New York: Frederick Ungar Publishing Company, Inc., 1960, p. 343.

soul sat hungrily at their table; unlike them, I was not trained to consider awareness as easy as cracking nuts." [18]

The poet Ranier Maria Rilke is the literary prophet of Nietzsche. In Rilke, and to a certain extent in his predecessor Hölderlin, we see the "religious" reconstruction of self-awareness after the destruction of God by Nietzsche. But the program is distinctively different from that of the rationalists. The Romantic movement in England and the Aüfklarung in Germany represent literary movements expressive of the rationalistic temper of the time. It is no coincidence, for example, that Shelley found his mythic prototype in Prometheus, the defiant one, the one who brought fire and technic to man. Rilke, following in the wake of Nietzsche, finds his mythic prototype in Orpheus, the singer of songs in hell. Whereas Shelley was the social visionary, leading man in ever-greater triumphs over ignorance and injustice, Rilke more modestly proposed to lift man by the sheer power of poetry itself. God is dead; justice is improbable; only immanence remains. In one of his letters, Rilke noted that "God is the no longer sayable; and his attributes fly back into creation."

The Church's Reaction

These then are two options for the definition of modern man. He may be utopian, post-Christian, rationalist, or he may choose to be nihilistic, post-Christian, existentialist. The irony of the case is that each is possible of a "religious" statement. There can be little question about the authority in the world of Julian Huxley's *Religion Without Revelation,* on the one hand, or Camus' *The Rebel,* on the other. They are influential and informed religious statements. That they pose a desperate challenge to traditional Christianity is not to be denied, and to that challenge and response we must now turn.

The irony of the Church's dilemma is to be seen in the fact that while the Church has thought that its cultural destiny lay more

[18] New York: Boni and Liveright, Inc., 1917, p. 145.

obviously with the cultural affirmers—in the tradition of the Enlightenment—it is with the irrationalists, the existentialist critics, that the most vital religious thrusts may be seen in our time. While both the rationalists and the irrationalists have rejected classical Christian theological positions, they continue to operate more or less within the framework of an ethical system established by Christianity. Thus you find the ethical absolutism and perfectionism of Lord Russell on the one hand, and the moral rigorism of Camus on the other. Henri Peyre of Yale has noted that the French existentialists are really Jansenists—even, in Peyre's phrase, "Sunday school teachers turned inside out." The vigor with which Lord Russell speaks out on the moral aspects of nuclear testing and Camus or Koestler on capital punishment is an indication of the moral stance of these positions. If God is dead, then any sense and meaning in human community or personal existence must become a human responsibility. Therefore, in Camus a deeply compelling humanism presents itself to modern Western man who has despaired of traditional concepts of God and man. The same is true with the rationalist, who is humanistic moralist because rational categories may provide the structure for moral behavior, indeed they must if revelation is irrelevant.

Just as the modern artist must draw upon biblical allusion and apocalyptic symbol to communicate a criticism of Christianity in our time, so also must the moralist draw heavily upon the vested humanistic traditions of Christian history. The point at which the Church is often oblivious to the extent of the post-Christian mood of our culture is its inability to challenge the atheist to acknowledge his Christian roots, on the one hand, and its failure often to affirm moral leadership in the cultural crisis on the other. We in The Methodist Church in North America feel this most painfully when we realize that such secular institutions as education, professional athletics, and the military establishment have often acted with more dispatch and with more decisiveness in the matter of racial exclusion than has The Methodist Church. The tragedy is that the Church is generally responsible for both conditions. Its ethic makes inevitable the reconstruction of human society without regard to race, and the preaching of the Church insures the ultimate triumph of this ideal. On the other hand, the Church as institution in a segregated society acts with more conservative response and finds itself being judged by its own ideal.

In the MESTA study, Professor Schilling has noted the fact that Methodist people generally see little correlation between their beliefs as Methodist Christians and motivation and guidance for positive social living.[19] This disparity between profession and confession is one of the most serious drawbacks in the image of the Church in the modern world. C. E. M. Joad, the colorful English critic of Christianity and later a convert to it, once remarked that "the Anglican Church [is] a piece of machinery which continues to function in order to produce a commodity which nobody wants, through sheer inability to stop." [20] My personal judgment is that The Methodist Church is in grave danger of this very problem. On a variety of fronts, our churches are committed to no struggles. We are being outflanked by the secular moralist; we are being challenged by the imaginative artists; we are being confounded by the biblical and Christian traditions which we are in danger of no longer being able to identify.

What Is the Church to Do?

Several suggestions have been advanced as a program for the Church in this so-called post-Christian era. They are, however, fragmentary and tentative. For example, Paul Tillich suggested in his Terry Lectures at Yale in 1951 that we need to look for the "God beyond God." He has given us tantalizingly little help in this definition, but we might say that Tillich's whole apologetic method points us toward an answer. He is interested in correlating man's existential questions with the answers of the Christian faith. As I understand this method, it intends to answer the *real* ques-

[19] *Methodism and Society in Theological Perspective* (Nashville: Abingdon Press, 1960), III, 169.

[20] *Guide to Modern Wickedness* (Toronto: Ryerson Press, 1939), p. 61.

tions rather than hypothetical ones. In this system, Tillich has made a very great contribution to the Church's apologetic. In America, his interest in and support of the psychoanalytic movement and its relation to the Christian faith has been immensely helpful.

Another currently vogue response is that suggested by some fragments from Dietrich Bonhoeffer. He wrote:

The attack by Christian apologetic upon the adulthood of the world I consider to be in the first place pointless, in the second ignoble, and in the third un-Christian. Pointless, because it looks to me like an attempt to put grown-up man back into adolescence, i.e. to make him dependent on things on which he is not in fact dependent any more, thrusting him back into the midst of problems which are in fact not problems for him any more. Ignoble, because this amounts to an effort to exploit the weakness of man for purposes alien to him and not freely subscribed to by him. Un-Christian, because Christ himself is being substituted one particular stage in the religiousness of man, i.e. human law.[21]

"Religionless Christianity," divestment of institutional order and traditional modes of operation, is apparently Bonhoeffer's suggestion. He asks the very serious question whether this new man needs the Church as institution at all. Experiments like the famous, ill-fated worker priest movement in France illustrate such experimentation.

Both Bonhoeffer and Tillich, and indeed all other serious statements in this matter, ask the basic question: "Was not the God that died merely an inadequate and incomplete statement of the God that is, and is not the institution of the Church too much involved in the dead God and in desperate need of the God that is?" At this point it occurs to me that the Methodist people have a real contribution to make. We must, as a Church, insist upon the primacy of those things which make us a people of God—scripture, sacrament, preaching—but we must also be free from any hesitation or reluctance to prevent us from wrestling with the

[21] *Prisoner for God: Letters and Papers from Prison,* June 8, 1944 (New York: The Macmillan Company, 1953), p. 147.

problems and challenges to the world about us, even the problem of religious language. Wesley created a new language with his hymns!

Wesley was a kind of eighteenth-century Bonhoeffer. He combined scriptural holiness with prudential judgment regarding the Church's program. Rather than agonize over the peculiar ambiguities we find ourselves in—as a denomination—we should rejoice, for Methodism—to borrow Bonhoeffer's famous phrase—was at the "centre of the village" and not on the "borders" where human powers give out. What was of divine institution was *essential.* All else was *prudential.* The class meeting, the bands, lay preachers, open-air preaching, even the ordination of Coke—these were imaginative and correct responses to the human and social situation in the eighteenth century. In his *Plain Account of the People Called Methodists,* Wesley describes an ecumenical emphasis—one evening a month he allotted to the reading of accounts "of the work God is carrying on in the earth . . . , not among us alone, but among those of various opinions and denominations."

Methodism is uniquely blessed, by our founder's style, in that it may, through its emphasis on the essentials of faith, speak to the permanent condition of man as man. Through its style, its prudential experimentation with the methods of evangelism, it may be able to speak to that which is the peculiar self-understanding of man in our time.

BIBLIOGRAPHY

Baumer, Franklin. *Religion and the Rise of Skepticism.* New York: Harcourt, Brace and World, Inc., 1960.

Bonhoeffer, Dietrich. *Prisoner for God: Letters and Papers from Prison.* New York: The Macmillan Company, 1954.

Elmen, Paul. *The Restoration of Meaning in Contemporary Life.* Garden City, N.Y.: Doubleday & Company, Inc., 1958.

Guardini, Romano. *The End of the Modern World.* Translated by Joseph Theman and Herbert Burke. London: Sheed & Ward, Ltd., 1956.

Jaspers, Karl. *Man in the Modern Age.* Garden City, N.Y.: Doubleday & Company, Inc., 1957.

Jenkins, Daniel. *Beyond Religion*. Philadelphia: Westminster Press, 1962.
Smith, Ronald Gregor. *The New Man*. New York: Harper & Brothers, 1956.
Thieliche, Helmut. *Nihilism: Its Origin and Nature with Christian Answer*. New York: Harper & Row, Publishers, 1961.
Vahanian, Gabriel. *The Death of God*. New York: George Braziller, Inc., 1961.